INSTITUTE OF
BRILLIANT
FAILURES

PAUL LOUIS ISKE

INSTITUTE OF BRILLIANT FAILURES

MAKE ROOM TO EXPERIMENT, INNOVATE, AND LEARN

Business Contact *Publishers*

Amsterdam/Antwerp

© 2019 Paul Louis Iske
Business Contact Publishers
Original title *Instituut voor Briljante Mislukkingen*
Translated by Maud Bovelander
Cover and interior design Adept Vormgeving
Visuals Johan van der Woude
Author photo Arnold Reyneveld
Printer Wilco

ISBN 978 90 470 1231 3

www.businesscontact.nl

TABLE OF CONTENTS

Foreword   5

Introduction   7

1. An Introduction to Brilliant Failures

A Call for Less Caution   13

So What Exactly is a Brilliant Failure?   14

Brilliant Failures as Part of Life   17

The BriFa Model: Positive Change Through Trying and Learning   27

Applying Chapter 1   33

2. Failure Is in Our DNA

Reality Often Turns Out Differently Than Expected   35

The Dirty Dozen   38

Creativity   43

Theory U: Changing and Being Open to Failure   44

Applying Chapter 2   49

3. Complexity as a Cause of Failing Brilliantly

Complicated Systems   51

Complex Systems   52

Complex Adaptive Systems   59

Our World Has Truly Become Much More Complex   60

Complexity in Projects and Programs   62

Applying Chapter 3   67

4. A Favorable Climate for Innovation and Entrepreneurship

Innovation   69

Open Innovation: An Additional Layer of Complexity   74

Entrepreneurship Is a Process of Trial and Error   76

Applying Chapter 4   85

5. A Common Language: Archetypes

Pattern Recognition 88

Patterns in Failing Brilliantly: Sixteen Archetypes 90

Failing and Learning at Various Levels 119

Applying Chapter 5 122

6. On knowledge and Learning

Knowledge Makes the World Go Round 125

The Knowledge Value Chain 126

Knowledge Transfer 129

Various Levels of Learning: Single-Loop and Double-Loop Learning 132

Failing and Learning in the World of Science and Research 138

Applying Chapter 6 144

7. Scenarios: Learning from Brilliant Failures Before They Happen

Alternative History 146

Alternative Future 147

Scenarios: Learning from the Future 148

War-Gaming: Failing Brilliantly in the Future 157

Applying Chapter 7 160

8. The Importance of a Safe Environment

The Influence of the Environment 162

Biomimicry: What We Can Learn from Nature 165

Serious Optimism 168

Applying Chapter 8 173

9. The Influence of Culture on Failing Brilliantly

On Culture 175

Brilliant Failures in the Netherlands Compared to Other Countries 177

Failure in the Context of Government 193

Applying Chapter 9 202

10. The Institute of Brilliant Failures (IoBF)

The IoBF Knowledge Environment: BriFa Learning Environment   204
IoBF Intervention: Journal of Brilliant Failures   205
IoBF Intervention: Brilliant Failure Award   206
IoBF Intervention: "Awareness Climate" for Experimentation
and Learning   215
Applying Chapter 10   216

Acknowledgments   218
Guest authors   220
References   224

FOREWORD

People love stories; above all, stories that make sense. We interpret everything that happens around us in the context of subjective mental constructs—stories or "narratives"—that we develop throughout our lives, outside of our conscious awareness. And if these narratives are inconsistent with the facts, we are not very likely to adapt our narratives to the facts. On the contrary, facts that don't fit into our stories are denied, disputed, or rationalized in such a way that the underlying narrative structure remains intact. It takes time and effort for us to change our ways. This is how thought patterns, theories and insights that have long proven vulnerable to the cleansing power of facts may nonetheless persist for a long time, often implicitly and subliminally.

One of these persistent narratives concerns the way people, organizations, products/services, and insights evolve and improve. Long story short, this narrative is as follows: If all goes well, everything is balanced and runs like a well-oiled machine within the bounds of possibility. This equilibrium is the starting point from which people and organizations seek improvement. First you determine what is necessary and possible, then you carefully map out the change, and finally you successfully implement the innovation. In this way, the "system" moves from equilibrium to equilibrium, carefully planned and well thought out. This narrative leaves little, if any, room for trial and error. Mistakes are almost always seen as avoidable and culpable. In this worldview, they tend to be seen as the result of intellectual laziness in the initial phase or carelessness and errors in the implementation phase.

If you stop to think about it for a moment, you'll realize just how pervasive this way of thinking is in many social processes. Mistakes always require that someone takes the blame or gets fired, leaving a permanent blemish on their resume. Costs resulting from unsuccessful experiments are considered a waste of money. Decisions must be recorded and justified in advance with absolute bureaucratic perfection, as if all necessary information is known in advance and leaders are able to predict the future. The effects of "equilibrium thinking" can also be observed in economic theory, the basis for so much policy: The economy is usually seen as being out of equilibrium, but tending toward it.

The real world, however, is messier and less clear than the above makes it seem; and it always will be. This is a fundamental fact of existence. Almost all decisions must be made based on incomplete information. Circumstances are always changing, and many things are completely unpredictable. Everything—people, organizations, countries, even nature itself—is constantly in transition. In such circumstances, the command-and-control approach is of limited use. Greater emphasis is placed on learning through frequent experimentation. Trial and error, in other words. It's virtually impossible to know everything in advance and absolutely impossible to predict the future, so we'll have to learn by trying. The human mind actually evolved to prefer this way of learning, where failure is considered as valuable as success, if not more than. This intuitively doesn't feel right to many people, especially because it's not what they've been taught. One might reasonably argue that people surely shouldn't be asked to start experimenting left and right, only to celebrate when their project predictably goes sideways. But experiments can be designed in such a way that they add a lot of value, even if they fail. These are the Brilliant Failures this book is about. We need to change our way of thinking about experiments and failures, and this book contributes greatly to that end. It presents a systematic framework of thought, that is, an alternative narrative to the joyless and rigid narrative summarized above. And it does so in a way that can be considered positive and even cheerful. It's exactly what we need.

Dr. T.B.P.M. Tjin-A-Tsoi
Director General
Statistics Netherlands (CBS)

INTRODUCTION

Ever since childhood, I've been fascinated by knowledge, particularly the progress of mankind as a result of the development and effective application of knowledge. During my studies and doctoral research in theoretical physics, I developed a passion for understanding complex systems. I studied topics in the field of statistical physics, which attempt to understand the behavior of systems consisting of many parts. However, I discovered an even greater challenge: understanding systems in which *people* influence each other rather than molecules or elementary particles. Although people can achieve many great things together, they can also create less pleasant environments to be in. Sometimes they do so on purpose and sometimes it's a case of "organized stupidity"; that is, us making it unnecessarily difficult for ourselves to get the most out of ourselves and each other.

In a system in which we focus only on success and sweep everything that doesn't work under the rug, we've essentially trapped ourselves in such an environment of organized stupidity. This is a missed opportunity. Business schools and entrepreneurship programs, business incubators, entrepreneur awards: they all prioritize success, growth, unicorns, slick pitches, prizes, etc. The truth is that over 90 percent of new initiatives don't make it. Reason enough to prepare people for lack of success while still encouraging them to keep trying, and—if they don't succeed—to be proud of their efforts and apply the lessons learned in the future, whatever their plans may be. But that's often not what happens.

Success and happiness also tend to prevail in the "perfect world" presented on "not-so-social" media, which often causes feelings of inadequacy in young people. The consequences are well known: There's an alarming increase in young people suffering from stress, burnout, depression and loneliness, primarily because of the pressure they feel to perform.

At the many conferences and other meetings I've attended in my career, the world also seems to consist of a series of successes. It's just like the timeline of your average Facebook or Instagram account. Even in "serious" networks, such as academic networks, people prefer to report on successful activities, and "likes", that is citations. count heavily toward the evaluation of someone's achievements. The truth is that constantly emphasizing successes and omitting failures has nothing to do with reality.

Public debate started in the Netherlands around 2005 over the way we treat people who've gone bankrupt—the ultimate failure in the business world. Research had already shown that under certain conditions, people who went bankrupt in a "brilliant" way, i.e., not a particularly stupid and definitely not a criminal way, have a better chance of success the second time around than first-time entrepreneurs. This actually makes sense: They have experience and show perseverance. But the people around them often don't see it that way. People who fail are pitied or no longer trusted, or both. This is not exactly constructive. And it doesn't just apply to people who've failed in the business world either. You can fail in your personal life, in academia, the arts, sports... In fact, failure may lurk around just about every corner.

I was once responsible for ABN AMRO Bank's Dialogues Incubator, an innovation platform focused on creating more disruptive, sustainable business models and open innovation. There were a few successes, but many of these businesses were ultimately unsuccessful. This wasn't a problem: the Institute of Brilliant Failures could always use them as case studies! (This is what they call "hedging" in the world of finance.)

I'd already started wondering how one might go about creating an environment in which people find it perfectly natural to learn from their failed activities and subsequently share the lessons they learned with others in order to prevent them from running into the same problems. This led to the founding of the Institute of Brilliant Failures, which attempts to answer such questions as: what is the difference between a mistake and a Brilliant Failure? How can we learn from failures? How do you create an environment in which people and organizations feel free to experiment, even if results cannot be guaranteed? How do you take away the fear of admitting and learning from mistakes? And how can failed activities become easier to recognize and communicate to others?

Everyone knows that getting knocked down and getting up again is part of life. Can't we use this to our advantage and learn from each other, rather than just bragging about our successes? What if knowledge acquired through trial and error can benefit not only you, but also the people around you? A failure could suddenly become very valuable and may well turn out to be a Brilliant Failure.

We can't change the past, but we should strive to use past insights and ideas in new attempts as much as possible. This is what failing brilliantly is all about. The way ahead usually isn't a straight highway like Route 66 through Monument Valley; it's a winding road, sometimes no more than a trail, through a varied landscape. People who only drive on automatic pilot on Route 66 miss out on much of real life. This book is intended to serve as a navigation system for the road map of real life, in which people who've taken a wrong turn—as we all regularly do—may still end up at the most beautiful destinations.

My goal is to take away the feelings of fear and shame associated with failure. I'd like to see them replaced with a sense of pride in trying, and a sense of enrichment derived from the lessons that can be learned, shared, and applied.

Because there's so much to be said about failing and failing brilliantly, and we want to share as much information with you as possible and as clearly as possible, we've used symbols to indicate parts of the text that add to or expand on the main text:

Indicates an example of a Brilliant Failure

Indicates a concept or a theoretical foundation or digression

Indicates a guest author's contribution

1. AN INTRODUCTION TO BRILLIANT FAILURES

Let's get right to the main point of this book: Daring to fail is important! If no one dared to take any risks anymore, things would go downhill fast. Failure is inevitable, even necessary, for society to progress. This is why we should stimulate enterprising people and organizations that aren't afraid to try something new and to face the consequences. Because, let's be honest—where would the world be without courage, without the opportunity to learn from things that don't go according to plan, without serendipitous discoveries?

A Call for Less Caution
Everyone can contribute to reducing caution and increasing acceptance of failure. This applies first and foremost to legislators, policy makers, social partners and senior managers. They have the power to simplify regulation and turn penalties for failure into positive incentives for sticking one's neck out. The media can also play an important role by reporting on the positive aspects of failure. But "be the change you wish to see in the world" applies here as well. Ultimately, everyone could give themselves and the people around them more room to experiment and to accept and share mistakes and failures.

The Institute of Brilliant Failures (IOBF) gathers knowledge that can be used to clear the way for new experiences, innovation and enterprises and to increase the learning potential of people, organizations, and society as a whole. Just to be clear, we do encourage people to stick their necks out every now and then, but we don't advocate irresponsible risk-taking. While wandering onto the highway blindfolded is adventurous, it doesn't fall within the scope of the IOBF. Yes, the possible (or probable) confrontation with oncoming traffic would be a failure, but certainly not a *Brilliant* Failure!

So What Exactly is a Brilliant Failure?

There are a great many situations that may turn out differently than expected, both in business and in private life. These kinds of situations tend to arise when we were trying to do something right, not when we were acting foolishly or selfishly. But when exactly is a failure not simply a failure, but a Brilliant Failure? We'll be using the following definition:

A *Brilliant Failure*© is an attempt to create value whose originally intended result isn't achieved, despite the fact that no avoidable or culpable mistakes were made. Lessons were learned and learning experiences are shared.

The word "failure" suggests an unsatisfactory outcome—something you'd probably rather not talk about. The opposite is true of Brilliant Failures: They're the kinds of failures you'll be itching to talk about! The result obtained through a Brilliant Failure may not be the intended result, but it does have value. It might even be more valuable than originally intended. We distinguish two types of Brilliant Failures, based on their outcome:

- Type 1, whose result is different than intended but still valuable, sometimes even more valuable than the intended result.
- Type 2, whose result is less valuable than originally intended, but does provide a learning experience.

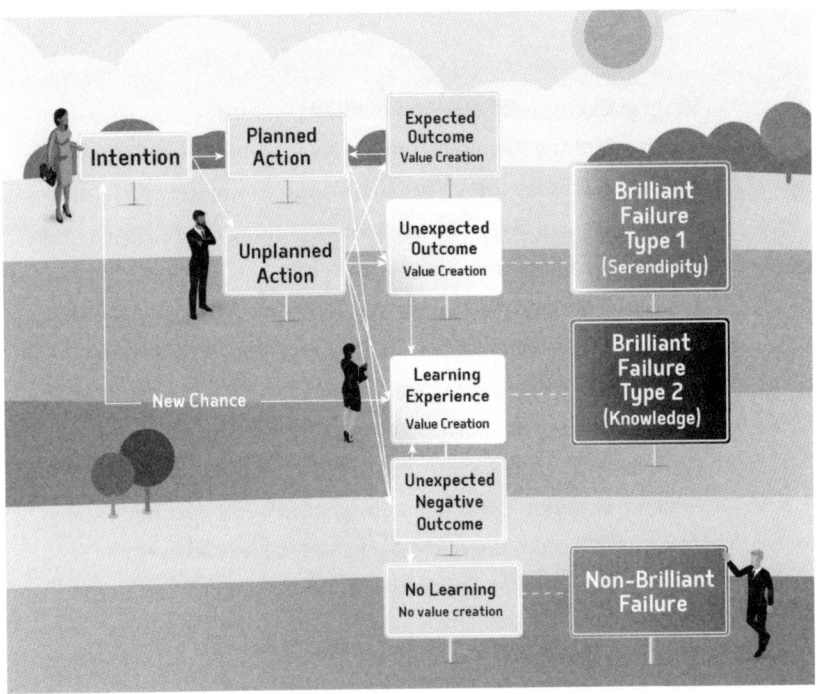

Figure 1. Different types of Brilliant Failures

A Type 1 Brilliant Failure often involves serendipity; discovering something important by chance. To quote the definition favored by Pek van Andel, who's done much research in this area, "Serendipity is looking for a needle in a haystack and finding the farmer's daughter." Accidentally making a mistake (unplanned action) can also be a brilliant failure, as it might result in a different desirable outcome or a valuable learning experience. In some cases, it's actually useful to make a mistake because it may lead to new insights and progress. Think, for example, of the board game Mastermind: you can choose to create a combination you know to be incorrect in order to acquire new information.[1]

---

1 The book *Brilliant Mistakes* (2011) by Paul Schoemaker is about these kinds of mistakes, which are sometimes deliberately made to discover a way forward.

Viagra: Example of a Type 1 Brilliant Failure

There are many examples of innovations that are essentially a by-product of a search for something completely different. Viagra is one of them. Pharmaceutical company Pfizer set out to develop a treatment for heart failure and angina pectoris. Developing a new drug is a risky, long, and expensive process that may be influenced by many different factors, such as unexpected side effects, problems in scaling up production, poor efficacy or new alternatives. In this case, the drug turned out to have a side effect on about half of the subjects —which was actually much appreciated by their other halves. The rest is history: Seven Viagra tablets are sold every second, and not only to people with cardiovascular problems.

Brilliant Failures don't have to be as spectacular as the Viagra example to be worthwhile, though. As mentioned earlier, learning potential plays an important role in determining whether a failure is brilliant or simply a failure. Value creation takes place even in situations where the result itself has no value, but learning has occurred. The knowledge acquired may be directly or indirectly applicable. We may learn that something doesn't work, in which case we might just try again. As Edison said, "I didn't fail a thousand times; the light bulb was an invention with a thousand steps." Even a mistake—that is to say, a failure that could theoretically have been avoided—can be upgraded to a Brilliant Failure if there is sufficient value creation based on the knowledge gained.

In the Institute, we've introduced the "BriFa score" ("Brilliant Failure score") to indicate how brilliant a failure is. The resulting acronym VIRAL also happens to be a useful mnemonic to remind you that Brilliant Failures deserve to be spread because everyone can learn from them. In other words, they're something to be proud of.

$$\text{BriFa-score} = V \times I \times R \times A \times L$$

Each variable in this formula can take on a value from 0 to 1:

V =   vision (V is 0 for an attempt at something completely useless, such as jumping off the Eiffel Tower to see if gravity still exists, and V is equal to 1 for an attempt whose intended goal justifies the effort, such as an attempt to solve a long-standing armed conflict),

I =   inspiration (or commitment, the degree to which someone is actually prepared to make the necessary effort),

R =   risk management (the extent to which risks have been identified and accepted or dealt with. R is 0 if someone has not considered the risks at all, is taking irresponsible risks, or being unnecessarily risk averse),

A =   approach (the extent to which the right resources and knowledge are being used) and

L =   learning experiences (the extent to which knowledge has been developed and made usable or reusable).

The BriFa score is a useful tool in discussing just how brilliant a failure actually is. We also use it in the judging process of the Brilliant Failure Awards, which you can read more about in Chapter 10.

Brilliant Failures as Part of Life
As individuals, we try to give meaning to our lives in a complex and changeable world. We do this partially alone and partially with the people we love, our family and friends, or our colleagues. Some things work out and others don't. It's really quite natural.

> *Life is what happens while you are busy making other plans.*
>
> JOHN LENNON

Below are a few examples of situations in which we may succeed but may just as easily fail, no matter how hard we try.

- Establishing personal relationships. Although most people enter into relationships with good intentions, long-term commitment proves to be a challenge in many cases.
- Engaging in personal endeavors, such as going on vacation, moving, or emigrating.
- Taking a course, learning to play an instrument, and so on. You go into it with an idea of what you want to achieve, but the reality often turns out to be different.
- Playing sports. Especially in competitive sports and when the level of ambition is high, success and failure are often two sides of the same coin. And if no one were to participate in sports unless they were guaranteed to win, there wouldn't be all that many players on the field.

Emigrating to New Zealand

The intention
Our department secretary had always loved New Zealand and decided to move there. Her main reasons for emigrating were the nature, the peace and quiet, and the adventure. She'd also met a nice guy from Auckland on vacation and wanted to get to know him better.

The approach
She quit her job, canceled her lease and bought a one-way ticket to Auckland. She found a job as a waitress at a fast-food restaurant and lodgings with an English family. She enrolled in a fashion design course.

The result
She returned eight months later, was rehired by our company and quickly became PA to one of the managers, responsible for our business in Oceania. She still loved New Zealand—but as a holiday destination. She'd missed her family and friends, and the guy from Auckland had quickly found himself a new girlfriend. The thrill of bungee jumping had worn off after a few goes. And the weather was nothing to write home about, either... Still, she'd enjoyed it and New Zealanders will always have a special place in her heart.

The lessons learned
Before leaving, she said, "I'd rather regret the things I've done than the things I haven't done!" Looking back, the experience also had a positive effect on her career and her personal life.

There are various reasons why people would rather not fail. First of all, not achieving something you want to achieve is always disappointing. This uncomfortable feeling is reinforced by worry about how others may react. People might think less of you if you fail to succeed. They may not hire you again, or they may make business transactions difficult. But it doesn't have to be that way, as the following example shows.

Johannes Haushofer's CV of Failures

Many people prefer not to talk about things that didn't work out for them—especially not at moments when they're supposed to promote themselves, such as in a job interview. Johannes Haushofer is Assistant Professor of Psychology at Princeton University. You don't get there without doing something right. But even a professor at Princeton can't succeed at everything. In fact, there are many things Haushofer didn't succeed at. And he believes that, rather than sweeping them under the rug, we should tell others about our failures, because they show what we put a lot of energy into and learned a lot from.

JOHANNES HAUSHOFER
CV OF FAILURES

Most of what I try fails, but these failures are often invisible, while the successes are visible. I have noticed that this sometimes gives others the impression that most things work out for me. As a result, they are more likely to attribute their own failures to themselves, rather than the fact that the world is stochastic, applications are crapshoots, and selection committees and referees have bad days. This CV of Failures is an attempt to balance the record and provide some perspective.

This idea is not mine, but due to a wonderful article in *Nature* by **Melanie I. Stefan,** who is a Lecturer in the School of Biomedical Sciences at the University of Edinburgh. You can find her original article here, her website here, her publications here, and follow her on Twitter under *@MelanieIStefan.*

I am also not the first academic to post their CV of failures. Earlier examples are here, here, here, and here.

This CV is unlikely to be complete – it was written from memory and probably omits a lot of stuff. So if it's shorter than yours, it's likely because you have better memory, or because you're better at trying things than me.

Degree programs I did not get into

2008	PhD Program in Economics, Stockholm School of Economics
2003	Graduate Course in Medicine, Cambridge University
	Graduate Course in Medicine, UCL
	PhD Program in Psychology, Harvard University
	PhD Program in Neuroscience and Psychology, Stanford University
1999	BA in International Relations, London School of Economics

Academic positions and fellowships I did not get

2014	Harvard Kennedy School Assistant Professorship
	UC Berkeley Agricultural and Resource Economics Assistant Professorship
	MIT Brain & Cognitive Sciences Assistant Professorship
	This list is restricted to institutions where I had campus visits; the list of places where I had first-round interviews but wasn't invited for a campus visit, and where I wasn't invited to interview in the first place, is much longer and I will write it up when I get a chance. The list also shrouds the fact that I didn't apply to most of the top economics departments (Harvard, MIT, Yale, Stanford, Princeton, Chicago, Berkeley, LSE) because one of my advisors felt they could not write a strong letter for them.

Figure 2. Johannes Haushofer's CV of Failures

That's why Haushofer wrote his "CV of Failures," a chronological account of everything at which he didn't succeed. His eventual success didn't come *despite* his failures, but *because* of these learning experiences. For example, his articles getting rejected taught him how to send in articles with a better chance of acceptance. Note the meta-failure at the end: "This darn CV of Failures has received way more attention than my entire body of academic work."

Failing in organizations

Modern organizations have to keep changing and improving in order to remain successful. This requires a strategy and a corporate culture with enough room for experimentation and learning. According to strategic management guru Igor Ansoff (2007), uncertainty limits people and organizations in their ability to plan ahead. The more uncertainty, then, the greater the need for what he calls "proactive flexibility," the ability to react before others do and to deal with unexpected results and the rapid changeability of our environment. To find your way in this day and age, navigating is increasingly more important than managing and controlling. And this is a skill that's acquired through experimenting, making mistakes, and adjusting course accordingly.

Michael Eisner, former CEO of The Walt Disney Company, was convinced that punishing failure invariably leads to mediocrity, as "mediocrity is what fearful people will always settle for."

Research has shown that having a higher tolerance for making mistakes within organizations pays off. For her PhD in Organization Sciences, Nicoletta Dimitrova (2014) investigated which strategy is more constructive in terms of perception by others and task performance: error prevention—trying to prevent all mistakes so as to avoid negative consequences, or error management—accepting the fact that mistakes will be made and minimizing their negative consequences.

Many managers are afraid to use error management as a strategy because they think it might negatively affect their reputation. According to Dimitrova, this fear is unfounded. In fact, leaders who primarily view mistakes as learning experiences are seen as more likable, moral and competent than leaders who opt for an error prevention strategy. Moreover, they tend to inspire greater trust among their employees, who are more content with their leader and more motivated as compared to employees of leaders who adopt an error prevention strategy. An approach aimed at effectively dealing with mistakes—rather than being overly careful to prevent them—provides more focus, reduces feelings of fear, and leads to greater job satisfaction. As we'll see in Chapter 7, this positively affects job performance as well. These findings clearly show that error management is the preferred strategy.

Failing in sports

Success and failure are particularly close together in the sports world. As the band Queen put it in the song *We Are the Champions*, a staple at sporting events:

We are the champions
No time for losers

Failing or losing in sports hurts, but there are no winners without losers! Here, too, one can partly turn failure into something positive by considering the learning opportunities. By carefully analyzing where and when things went wrong, you can try to improve in those areas. Professional tennis player Stanislas Wawrinka can attest to this:

Stan Wawrinka

In 2013, Swiss tennis player Stanislas Wawrinka encountered Novak Djokovic in the fourth round of the Australian Open. Although he put up a good fight, Wawrinka finally lost to the eventual winner of the tournament in five sets. He was disappointed, of course, but at the same time he stated that the match had taught him a lot, which made him think he could significantly improve his game. To emphasize this, he had a Samuel Beckett quote tattooed on his forearm: "Ever tried, ever failed? No matter. Try again, fail again." The following year, Wawrinka beat Djokovic in the semi-finals and went on to win the tournament. The motto can also be found on his website.

This is an example of a Brilliant Failure of the archetype "The Winner Takes It All." In a competitive world, it's important for people and organizations to stay motivated to participate, even if ultimately there can only be one victor.

Of course, the attitude of one's social environment is also very important in dealing with failures. In the world of professional sports, everyone and everything is under a microscope. Failure is often met with ruthlessness and support can be lost in the blink of an eye. Especially in sports such as soccer, coaches often turn out to be misunderstood talents. It's not just the athletes themselves, but also their coaches who know better than anyone that success is only an inch away from failure.

Coaching and Failing Brilliantly
(Contribution by Martijn Westerop)

Coaches have a significant impact on the preparation for a performance, but little to no impact during the performance itself, as they're not allowed to go on the field to actively coach their pupils. But can a coach, who generally can't participate in the moment of performance, have a decisive (negative) influence on a professional athlete's performance? The following examples—now infamous moments in Dutch sports history—show that they certainly can.

The Historic Mistake That Cost Sven Kramer the Gold Medal
During the 10,000m speed skating event at the Vancouver 2010 Winter Olympics, Dutch ice skater and hot favorite Sven Kramer was directed into the wrong lane by his coach Gerard Kemkers and disqualified as a result. His Olympic dream was shattered. It was a particularly bitter pill to swallow because the Olympic Games only take place every four years. Kramer failed to seize what was likely his last chance to correct the mistake: He finished sixth at the 2018 Winter Olympics in South Korea.

Kramer did, however, receive more international attention and appreciation for his achievements after the incident. In many countries, watching a 10,000m speed skating event is considered to be about as exciting as watching paint dry. This was spectacle and emotion, with a hero who was simultaneously an antihero—a human being. People appreciate that. As for Kemkers, he said, "The lesson I learned was that a coach has his limits. The team had ten medal candidates who all deserved attention, but there wasn't enough time." After Vancouver 2010, Kemkers created more time, space and energy for himself, for example by delegating much more.

He now gives lectures and workshops on dealing with successes as well as disappointments in professional sports.

The Single Worst Substitution Ever
Portugal, Euro 2004. After a lucky 1-1 draw against Germany, the Dutch soccer team needed a good result against the Czech Republic, who had won their first game.

The game was largely dominated by winger Arjen Robben, who'd recovered just in time for the Championship. Seemingly unstoppable, he'd already given two assists for the 2-1 lead. In the fifty-eighth minute, Netherlands national coach Dick Advocaat decided to withdraw Robben—to the utter consternation of Dutch people everywhere—and replace him with a defensive midfielder to guard the lead. It was a disaster. The Czech Republic brought the game to 2-2, a Dutch player was sent off with a red card, and the Czech Republic scored another goal two minutes before time.

Afterward, there was only one question on everyone's minds: Why on earth did Advocaat take Robben off the field? In the face of all the criticism, Advocaat had assistant coach Willem van Hanegem do the post-game press conference. When asked what he would do if Advocaat made a decision like this again, the assistant coach said, "I'd punch him out."

The tricky thing is that in this case, we'll never know what would have happened if Advocaat hadn't substituted Robben. This is often the problem with decisions that backfire and come under criticism.

Doing things differently in soccer

Spectator sports such as professional soccer cause simple, straightforward reactions in the outside world. If they win, the players get a pat on the back—but they better watch their backs if they lose... The well-known Dutch soccer coach, Foppe de Haan, subscribes to a different definition of success than just winning. To him, success is about improvement. Success is the team improving its play or its ability to work together, attack, or defend. Success is a player improving their technique of outmaneuvering a striker.

"The final result is simply the sum of all these factors. Don't ever say 'I want to be champion,' because you should get better every day. Never set your goal too far out of reach. Soccer is chaos; players have to learn to deal with that. They're actually trained for it, because they play six times a week, which means they inevitably make an incredible number of mistakes. In a soccer game, mistakes often can't be corrected immediately, but they can be corrected a little while later. The coach plays a major role in this. A coach who immediately expresses anger after a mistake, for example by swearing—soon discovers that doesn't work. As a coach, that's the moment to calm the player down so they can get on with their task," Foppe de Haan said in an interview with us. His view on failure is founded on his own background and experiences.

Foppe de Haan's career as a professional soccer coach kicked off when he became head coach of sc Heerenveen, a club that plays in the top division of professional soccer in the Netherlands. He also taught at the Netherlands Central Institute of Education for Sports Leaders (cios). Because of this, he was somewhat condescendingly characterized as "the teacher" in his capacity as coach. After three years he was "downgraded" to Head of Training at sc Heerenveen. Instead of considering this a failure, he decided to turn it around and think: Well, then I'll show them what a damn good teacher I am. Of course he needed a few months to recover mentally, but the new position eventually gave him a lot of energy and earned him much respect. The result: De Haan was rehired as head coach three and a half years later. By then, he'd settled into his position as Head of Training, and only accepted the position of head coach until someone else was found. He eventually became the longest-serving club coach in Dutch professional soccer, having coached sc Heerenveen for thirteen years. Under his guidance, the club qualified for a European club competition (the UEFA Cup Winners' Cup) for the first time in its history. De Haan later coached the Netherlands Under-21 team, winning the UEFA European U21 Championship twice and qualifying for the 2008 Summer Olympics in Beijing.

The BriFa Model: Positive Change Through Trying and Learning

This brings us to the core of this book: Failing Brilliantly is about positive change through trying and learning. We're primarily concerned with personal and collective growth. This kind of growth occurs when we create, share, and—above all—use knowledge while actually doing things; in the planning stage, the implementation phase, and afterward.

We've already introduced the BriFa score, which comprises five aspects whose first lettersform the acronym VIRAL. In the BriFa model, Brilliant Failures are the building blocks of learning processes. The central features of the BriFa model are the BriFa development spiral and the BriFa landscape in which people and organizations can develop themselves.

We'll first consider the kind of growth that is based on doing and learning. This development is schematically shown in Figure 3 at the next page. See how learning occurs during the various stages—before, during, and after— and how the path of learning is steepest during the action itself. Because of its shape, this kind of development is known as an S-curve. The speed of learning slows down at the end, which means it's time for the next process.

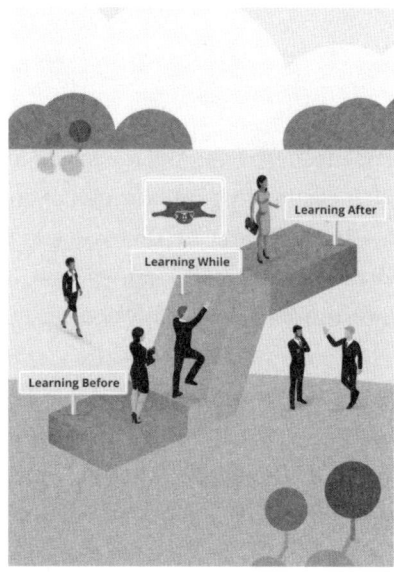

Figure 3. S-curve

The pattern of "planning, implementing, and completing" repeats itself, creating the image of a cyclical process in which the stage of completion is followed by a jump to the next learning process. Sometimes you have to go back a level to try again, and sometimes the knowledge acquired can be used directly in the next process. This kind of growth can be seen as a "spiraling" kind of growth: the BriFa learning spiral.

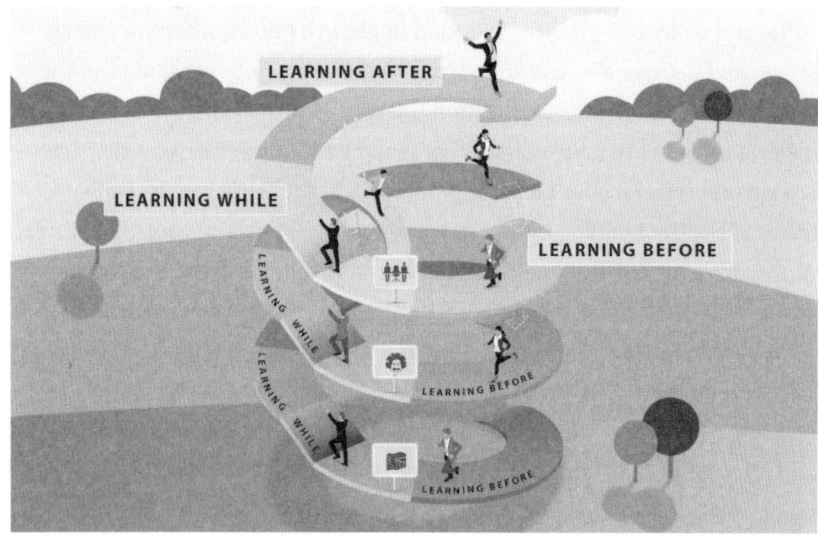

Figure 4. The BriFa growth spiral

This kind of growth may be individual, but it may also occur within families, teams, organizations, industries, or even society as a whole. Now imagine knowledge flowing freely from one context/environment/activity to the other. A large, evolving system will emerge, in which things that don't work gradually disappear and things that do produce positive results are absorbed into the system, resulting in the optimization of knowledge and continuous improvement. This is how we create an environment for learning from Brilliant Failures: the BriFa landscape. And this landscape for shared value creation and collective learning is a landscape we'll create together.

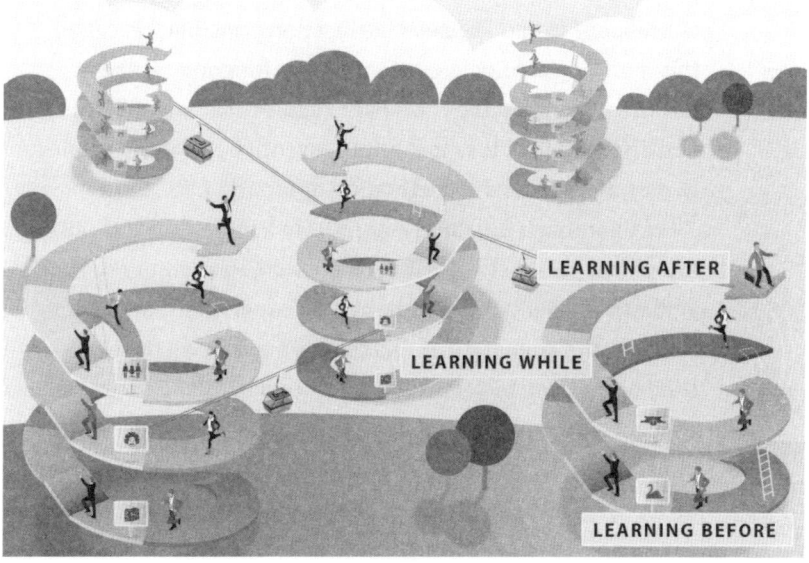

Figure 5. The BriFa landscape

This is an environment in which we move, experiment, experience, and learn! Knowledge is shared within and between contexts, and learning occurs both within and between the spirals. You learn from your own experiences as well as from others. Knowledge transfer can be promoted by applying a method that makes it easier to recognize Brilliant Failures and share them with others. This method is based on the use of so-called 'archetypes', frequently recurring patterns, which are shown in Figure 5 as "road signs" along the growth path. Chapter 5 will elaborate on these archetypes.

Philosophy as Failed Brilliance
Contribution by Henk Oosterling

What can be said about Brilliant Failures from a philosophical perspective? How does academic philosophy view failure? How do failures structure our thinking, which is generally characterized as brilliant? Is failure seen as a positive or a negative thing in philosophy? Perhaps the most obvious example of a philosophical gesture that makes failure the measure of brilliance is Karl Popper's falsification principle. He called this methodical principle a *sine qua non* for good research. But then, this isn't about Brilliant Failures that were identified after the fact. It's more about inventive counterexamples as part of a successful, methodical approach.

Let's approach Brilliant Failures from a more reflexive philosophical perspective. Is it even possible to attribute such an ambiguous quality to an initiative, an experiment, or a practice? For the ambiguity of this term is plain for all to see. In a tried-and-tested dialectical formula, two mutually exclusive concepts are grafted together into a single term. The reader, pulled back and forth between the positive and the negative meaning, is misled twice. Can something that is brilliant be a failure? Can a failure still be brilliant? Don't the definitions of these two concepts cancel each other out? This procedure has been routinely used to make tangible the complexity of reality in the modern history of philosophy. In the sixties, for example, Herbert Marcuse spoke of "repressive tolerance." The first part of this term, *repressive*, precludes the second part, *tolerance*. But when the system is protested loudly and critically in strictly regulated demonstrations, the bureaucratically controlled way of protesting and the many rules that must be followed preemptively take the sting out of it. In a way, the demonstration confirms the repressive power of the system.

At first glance, the term "Brilliant Failure" appears to be cut from the same cloth. But something else is going on here. If we go further back in the history of philosophy, another perspective presents itself. The structure of such a term somewhat resembles the so-called Epimenides Paradox, formulated in ancient Crete by the philosopher of the same name. The paradox concerns the following statement: "Epimenides the Cretan says: All Cretans are liars." Is this statement true or false? Logically speaking, there seems to be no unambiguous answer to this question. After all, each answer turns into its opposite. If all Cretans are liars, Epimenides the Cretan's statement "All Cretans are liars" is a lie. But if that's a lie—or at least allows for the thought that there are Cretans who don't lie, but speak the truth—the statement turns into its opposite. In that case, what Epimenides says is true. But if that's true—and all Cretans are liars—the entire statement isn't true, and so on and so forth. It wasn't until the twentieth century that the complexity of this statement was fully appreciated. It's a problem of self-reference: the statement refers to itself within itself. The British philosopher Bertrand Russell understood that the entire statement actually contains two clauses, each of which has a separate truth value. The statement "Epimenides the Cretan says..." may be true, regardless of what it is he says. The statement "All Cretans lie" may also be true in itself. But combining the statements into a single sentence causes a logical short circuit, and the reader will get lost in their attempts to make sense of this ambiguous statement.

Both cases involve a kind of feedback loop; a short circuit occurs between two words or clauses. So, is this what happens with a Brilliant Failure? You do something, but—despite all efforts to bring it to a successful conclusion—it fails. The intended goal is not realized. Here, "realized" can also be interpreted in two ways: "to realize something" may mean "to achieve something," but it may also mean "to come to fully understand something." A Brilliant Failure includes both aspects, although the latter and the former don't occur at the same time. Looking back on a failed process, you'll see where you dropped the ball or misjudged things. In retrospect, from the comfortable vantage point of hindsight, such a failure—now considered in light of what happened afterward—may suddenly prove to be a prelude to something that is now very successful. What was once a simple failure now turns out to have been a brilliant, albeit premature, move. It was brilliant because now, looking back with knowledge you didn't have at the time, you can see that there were very different forces at work than you suspected back then. You only realize that now. Now, looking back and reassessing, knowing what you know now, it turns out to be the key to solving a problem that has only just shown itself in its full magnitude.

The term "Brilliant Failure" thus refers to a process that reflects itself through two time scales in a feedback loop. On the first scale, the experiment coincides with itself and fails: It can't be realized. On the second scale, it's recontextualized through self-reference and literally given a brand new meaning. Feedback loops make you realize something that gives failure a completely different meaning. With the benefit of hindsight, a failure may thus become brilliant.

Applying Chapter 1

1. Your resume undoubtedly contains a number of things you've done that you're proud of. But why don't you take a page out of Johannes Haushofer's book and mention your most important learning experiences as well? Update your resume, adding at least one Brilliant Failure. It'll immediately stand out, as it'll show courage and arouse curiosity. There's a good chance you'll get invited and that you will have an interesting conversation about where and why you went wrong. A perspective employer might really appreciate such an addition to your resume, which means it'd increase rather than reduce the chance you'll achieve your goal.

2. Many discoveries occur more or less by accident. This is called serendipity. Serendipity can only happen if you're open to the unplanned. Start a conversation with a stranger, visit a neighborhood or city you've never visited before, watch a TV program you've never watched before, listen to music of an artist or composer you've never listened to before, or do a Google search for a topic you've never actively explored. So? What's it like?

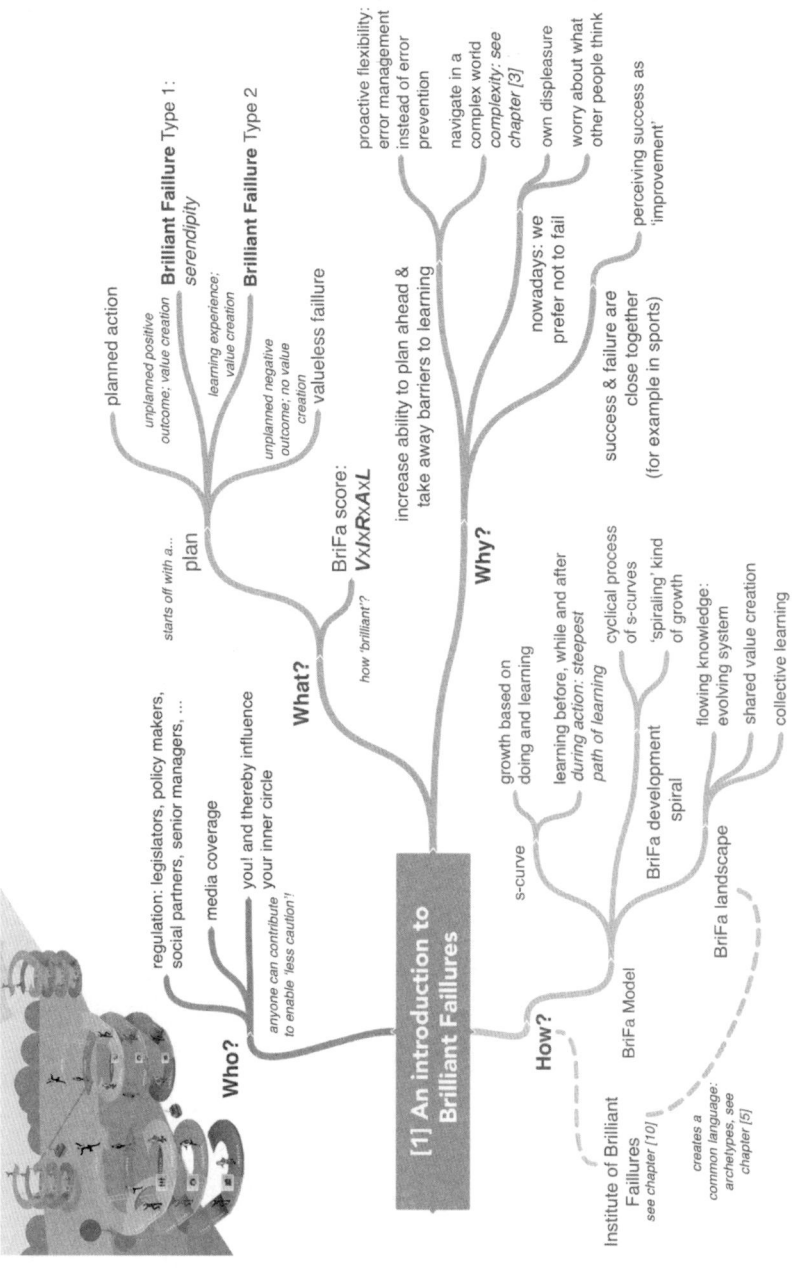

[1] An introduction to Brilliant Failures

Who?
anyone can contribute to enable 'less caution'!

- regulation: legislators, policy makers, social partners, senior managers, ...
- media coverage
- you! and thereby influence your inner circle

What?

- starts off with a.... plan
  - planned action
  - *unplanned positive outcome: value creation* — **Brilliant Faillure** Type 1: *serendipity*
  - *learning experience: value creation* — **Brilliant Faillure** Type 2
  - *unplanned negative outcome: no value creation*
  - valueless faillure
- *how 'brilliant'?* — BriFa score: $V \times I \times R \times A \times L$

Why?

- increase ability to plan ahead & take away barriers to learning
  - proactive flexibility: error management instead of error prevention
  - navigate in a complex world *complexity: see chapter [3]*
  - own displeasure
  - worry about what other people think
- nowadays: we prefer not to fail
- success & failure are close together (for example in sports)
- perceiving success as 'improvement'

How?

- s-curve
  - growth based on doing and learning
  - learning before, while and after *during action: steepest path of learning*
- BriFa development spiral
  - cyclical process of s-curves
  - 'spiraling' kind of growth
- BriFa landscape
  - flowing knowledge: evolving system
  - shared value creation
  - collective learning
- BriFa Model
- Institute of Brilliant Faillures *see chapter [10]*
- *creates a common language: archetypes, see chapter [5]*

2. FAILURE IS IN OUR DNA

Reality Often Turns Out Differently Than Expected

People who are serious about wanting to start a business usually develop a business plan or business case. But not everything in life goes according to plan—not by a long shot. Even the outcome of such a simple plan as buying a quart of milk at the grocery store can't be predicted with absolute certainty. You never know who or what you might run into on the way there! A business plan is not a perfect blueprint of the reality that will unfold along the way either. The heart of the matter is that "planning" often evokes the image of a straight path to the goal, but the reality is often different. You'll encounter unexpected circumstances, you'll find you didn't have all the information, matters will turn out to be more complicated than they appeared, the money will run out faster than expected, and so on.

Figure 6. The difference between a plan and reality

From Figure 6, we can conclude two things about many plans. Firstly, a straight line to the goal is not a realistic scenario. Secondly, there's more to experience and more to learn in reality than in the theoretical reality of the plan. The trick is not to strive too much for an "ideal" world, but to accept and appreciate the real world. It's exactly the unexpected things, the opportunities to learn from our experiences, and the difference between highs and lows that make life worth living!

The reason why reality is different from the image in Figure 6 is that life is simply more complex and complicated. More on that in Chapter 3. Let's start with ourselves—mankind.

People are a major reason why things tend to go differently than planned. It all starts with the way our brains work. We extrapolate. That is to say, we have expectations about what will happen based on previous experiences and information. Even if we resolve to take into account all possible outcomes, we often don't fully manage to do so. This is because the human brain isn't wired to switch off those expectations.

The brain is an institute of Brilliant Failures
Contribution by Ger Post

When we perceive something in our environment, our brain receives information about the perceived object (a house, a wolf, another person) from the senses. The simplest, crudest shapes are processed first, after which they're further combined and assembled into a meaningful representation of what's in front of us. Or, if we hear someone talking, the phonemes in their speech are combined into syllables, which together form words, then sentences, and finally ideas.

This is what researchers call the "bottom-up process," because perceptions are built up from below. The brain is a bit of a couch potato in this theory, only kicking in when a signal is received through the senses. But neuroscientific research has shown that neurons in the brain regularly communicate with each other, even when no signal is received from outside the brain. The bottom-up process, in other words, is not the only way our brain works.

For a decade, a growing number of scientists have been working on a new theory that includes a top-down process as well. This so-called "predictive processing" theory posits that our brains are constantly making predictions about our environment. It also posits (brace yourself!) that we primarily perceive these predictions, rather than reality. This may sound like a wild theory—especially when you learn that these researchers describe our perceptions as "controlled hallucinations" in which we don't perceive an incoming signal, but the *predictions* about the incoming signal.

So how come these hallucinations don't run away with us, at least in healthy people? According to predictive processing theory, the brain is constantly making countless top-down predictions about what is happening in our environment. At the same time, it receives bottom-up information about what is actually happening in the environment.

When these signals cross, the hypotheses of the brain are tested. A prediction may be accurate, but it may also be wrong. In the latter case, an "error signal" is generated. This error signal ensures that pre-existing ideas and the countless predictions derived from them come to be as close to reality as possible.

To reconcile the incoming signal with the prediction, and to reduce the error signal next time, the brain will adjust its expectations about the world so as to predict the situation more accurately in the future. This could be considered a Brilliant Failure: the prediction fails and is subsequently adjusted—something has been learned. These kinds of Brilliant Failures occur throughout the entire brain, from minute details in an image or sound to conceptual ideas about how the world works.

In addition to adjusting the preexisting idea or the predicti- ʹ
ons, there's another option: changing the environment. For
example, our bodies need to maintain a certain temperature
to stay alive. When we receive signals from our skin indica-
ting that our surrounding temperature is changing significantly, the brain doesn't change its internal model of body
temperature, but forces us to go find a warmer or cooler
place; it changes the environment to make the incoming signal better correspond to its expectations of the temperature.

The error signal, then, doesn't necessarily ensure that what
we learn is by definition "correct." Take, for example, one of
the major biases that affect our thinking: confirmation bias.
Confirmation bias is the tendency to look primarily for evidence for our beliefs, overlooking signals that indicate the
opposite. We actively seek proof of the correctness of our
world view so we won't have to adjust it. Or, as predictive
processing theory would put it: we adjust the world to our
view, rather than our view to the world.

The Dirty Dozen

Human behavior can be quite erratic and unpredictable. This is in part because of the way our brains work and in part because of our experiences
and the environment in which we developed. This section discusses a number of aspects of human behavior that are directly related to mistakes and
failures. A good starting point for this discussion are the so-called "Dirty
Dozen," the risks, psychological and behavioral factors that are responsible for accidents and incidents in the aviation industry. In this industry,
learning from mistakes and incidents is essential to ensure the safety of
passengers and crews and to keep improving safety. This is why each incident, whether major or minor, is thoroughly investigated and analyzed. The
Dirty Dozen are the result of decades of analyzing aviation accidents and
incidents worldwide. The intriguing, if somewhat disturbing, thing is that
many of these incidents could have been prevented—were it not for the

fact that they resulted from human weaknesses, which are the most difficult to overcome. The twelve human risk factors are:

1. Lack of communication
2. Complacency
3. Lack of knowledge
4. Distractions
5. Lack of teamwork
6. Fatigue
7. Lack of resources
8. Pressure
9. Lack of assertiveness
10. Stress
11. Lack of awareness
12. Norms

Some of the factors listed above are quite clearly capable of endangering
the safety of passengers and crews. Consider, for example, the effects of
lack of communication: Too often, communication is essentially a one-way
street. We send a message, assuming that it will be received and understood by the person on the other end. But we can't be sure of this without
checking it! To reduce this risk and avoid incorrect assumptions, the aviation industry makes use of written checklists and instructions. Having one
person read these out loud and the other person confirm them increases
the chances of both people understanding the message. Other industries
could learn from this.

And what of sleep-deprived people? A person who has been awake for
seventeen hours has the same thought and reaction skills as a person with
a blood alcohol level of 0.05 percent. That's the legal limit for driving under
the influence in many European countries. And pulling an all-nighter just
to finish that one project, for example, results in a degree of impairment
equivalent to a blood alcohol level of 0.1 percent. Fatigue, in other words,
seriously affects one's ability to make decisions. This is the reason why
pilots are only allowed to work a certain number of consecutive hours. But
regardless of your industry or line of work, the more tired you are the more
impaired your cognitive abilities and attention span.

So how about functioning in stressful situations? As stated previously, the human brain is always trying to reduce reality to recurring patterns in order to understand and be able to control things. When many things are happening at once, as is the case in complex situations, we tend to block out disruptive factors and shut ourselves off from these kinds of signals so as to focus on the matters right in front of us. This tendency is often exacerbated by stress. You can imagine that this might result in a fatal mistake in the event of an emergency in the cockpit, when a great deal of information has to be processed at the same time. But people can train themselves to continue to receive relevant signals. If you succeed in this, you can make an important contribution at the moment these signals occur. In other words, it's important to have people around you who are open to the unexpected in complex situations. Of course, this doesn't only apply to the aviation industry.

Perhaps one of the most dangerous Dirty Dozen factors is complacency, or (mental) laziness, because it's based on arrogance, pride, and the unwarranted confidence that one already has all the answers. This creates blind spots which mean we no longer recognize warning signs. When complacency has set in, we tend to stay in our comfort zone (the Canyon archetype), continue to see the world as we want to see it, and stop asking questions and challenging the status quo.

Pressure, and peer pressure in particular, also poses a serious risk. It can be so powerful that individuals feel compelled to align their opinions and wishes with those of the group. There's often a link with the factors "norms" and "assertiveness" here. Norms are also factors that influence individuals in making decisions they sometimes know to be wrong. When people lack assertiveness and are afraid to express their objections or concerns out of fear of being rejected, a situation may become dire. There are many examples of situations in which we do receive warnings, but allow ourselves to be influenced and consequently don't take the right action. Human psychological stress is understandable—it's one of the shortcomings of the human mind in a complex world—but complacency, peer pressure and norms are cultural phenomena. They're close to *hubris*, the word used by the ancient Greeks to describe excessive pride, overconfidence, megalomania, impudence and insolence, especially toward the Greek gods and/or the divine world order.

The good news is that once you're aware of these risk factors, you can use them to your advantage. Almost every one of these twelve factors can be turned around and turned into an opportunity.

Widerøe Flight 839, also known as the Værøy Accident
On April 12, 1990, at 2:44 p.m., a plane of Norwegian airline Widerøe crashed, killing all five people on board. The cause of the accident was a wind that exceeded the tolerance of the aircraft, causing the tail to break and the plane to become uncontrollable. The plane crashed 63 seconds after takeoff from Værøy Island, part of the Norwegian archipelago Lofoten. It took a few days for the wreck to be found.

Værøy Airport was known for its treacherous winds that regularly disrupted its flight schedule. The accident was investigated by the Accident Investigation Board, which concluded that the plane should never have been allowed to take off under the weather conditions at the time. So why did it? The plane had already been grounded for several days due to bad weather, and the pressure to finally leave was mounting, on the part of the passengers as well as the organization itself. It needed the aircraft for other flights. The pilot was eventually pressured into taking the risk, with a fatal outcome.

There was a combination of at least three Dirty Dozen factors at play here: pressure, norms (taking off in difficult weather conditions was considered ballsy) and lack of assertiveness.

According to the Accident Investigation Board, "The cause of the accident is that the plane during climb was subject to wind that succeeded the plane's construction criteria. This caused a crack in the tail rudder/tailplane causing the plane to become uncontrollable."

There also appeared to have been great pressure to leave despite the adverse weather conditions, partly because of the fact that this flight was the last one before Easter. Furthermore, the report condemned the fact that the location of the airport caused low regularity. Incidents at similar airports have led to knowledge that was not applied at Værøy. The Norwegian government decided to permanently close the airport; it was replaced with a heliport elsewhere on the island. By the way, it's interesting to mention that the norms at Widerøe Airlines changed as a result of the accident. Whereas pilots used to be admired for defying the elements (weather and wind), resisting commercial pressure is now considered brave.

Such fundamental changes in instructions and behavior are also the result of the deadliest accident in aviation history. On March 27, 1977, two Boeing 747s (one belonging to KLM, the other belonging to PanAm), collided on the runway on the Spanish island of Tenerife in the Canary Islands. 583 people died. As is often the case with accidents, this terrible crash was caused by an unfortunate combination of circumstances—bad weather, diverted flight routes, misunderstandings between air traffic control and the crews, and flawed radar and communication technology. But in addition to lack of communication, there was another Dirty Dozen factor at play here. The KLM co-pilot had indicated that he thought it irresponsible to take off. In the culture of the time, though, the captain had absolute say. He felt very pressured not to wait any longer and decided to take off anyway, with a fatal outcome. Partially as a result of this accident, the rule was established that if even just one crew member, cabin crew included, objects to departure, it is always a decisive argument to abort the procedure. This change has presumably prevented other accidents. Unfortunately, the learning experience came at a terrible price.

The lesson to be learned here is that people make mistakes, so organizations should operate under the assumption that even the best will make mistakes—always have at least two pilots on a flight, checklists, a lot of practice, and so on. This is how you ensure that mistakes are limited. But this only works if pilots and other crew members feel safe to report mistakes, so everyone can learn from them and the industry as a whole can become safer. For this reason, the aviation industry has agreed that flight recorders shouldn't be used in legal proceedings. Other industries, such as the healthcare industry, could use this as inspiration to create environments more conducive to making mistakes, learning, and improving safety. The results could be well worth it: for example, in 2017, there were zero accidents involving commercial jetliners.

Creativity

It's not just our weaknesses or bad luck that cause failures. One of our greatest qualities is our creativity, "the ability to generate new patterns by thinking multi-paradigmatically and seeing things from different perspectives." Creativity, in other words, is the ability to create something new. And creating something new means risking failure since you don't yet know whether your creation will work. Edward de Bono (1955) introduced various creative thinking techniques, including Provocative Operation (PO). This technique involves imagining things that aren't possible or allowed in reality. You'll end up in a situation where you've never been before as it's not possible or allowed in reality, but where you can get ideas that apply to the real world as well. A good example of provocative thinking concerns the qualities we usually associate with restaurants. One of these qualities may be service. If you "provoke" this idea ("PO Service"), you may arrive at the idea of a self-service restaurant, or home service, i.e. serving your own food. But we can take it much further: Can you imagine that there might be a valid reason for a restaurant with poor hygiene to exist? Well, imagine you've planned a trip to a country where the food contains certain bacteria to which you're not immune. You'd want to go to a restaurant with poor hygiene, whose food contains these bacteria in your own neighborhood. That way, you can be sick in the relative comfort of your own home, on paid leave, with your own doctor nearby. You can subsequently go on your trip immune to the bacteria. This may be just a hypothetical idea, but this theoretical Brilliant Failure does offer a few leads such as how to turn a disadvantage into an advantage. Failures, then, can also pave the way for new insights.

Clearly, there's often no direct correlation between the success or failure of a plan or idea and its inventor's "genius" or "stupidity." Did something recently go wrong in your life? Maybe you just breathed a sigh of relief, having safely concluded that the reasons were largely beyond your control. Apparently, luck isn't always what you make of it. And whether something is considered a success or a failure may also change over time.

History provides many examples of people who were misunderstood in their time. During his life, Van Gogh was largely misunderstood and lived in poverty; it was only after his death that his paintings became worth millions of dollars. Einstein didn't get stellar grades in university and was unable to find an academic position after graduating. He unsuccessfully applied for several jobs and had to start his career at the bottom of the ladder, as a substitute physics teacher. Fortunately, his rocky start didn't diminish his glorious finish—a fate not shared by the philosopher Socrates, unfortunately. Socrates is considered to be the first true philosopher of ancient Greece, but was accused of "corrupting the minds of the youth and denying the existence of the gods" and sentenced to death by poison. For all these kinds of examples, various accusations can be leveled against society or the "system" of the time. But taking the opposite view—that of the system—is equally interesting. How can you tell whether you're dealing with a genius or a madman? Asking people from different countries and states for their opinions on Donald Trump shows that such perceptions may vary dramatically.

Theory U: Changing and Being Open to Failure
The "risk" of failure brings uncertainty with it, and uncertainty is something we generally don't enjoy much. Still, we should dare to jump into the deep end to a certain extent. This seems very uncomfortable and counterintuitive to many organizations and individuals. Otto Scharmer's Theory U (2009) is a useful model that accurately describes how we can and should learn to think differently

What is Theory U?

Theory U is more than a theory; it's a process model of individual and organizational innovation and transformation. It involves several stages in which you "move down" to your inner place and then "move up" again to the change itself—hence the letter U. Theory U can help you turn the complex issues of our time into actual change by connecting with yourself and others, taking into account all relevant aspects of the issue. This process involves heightening the state of attention of those involved and using the wisdom of the unconscious. At the bottom of the U, the various aspects of the issue connect with your and other people's insights and lessons, providing the inspiration and ability to arrive at the solution through change. The U process makes learning from the future possible, in addition to learning from the past.

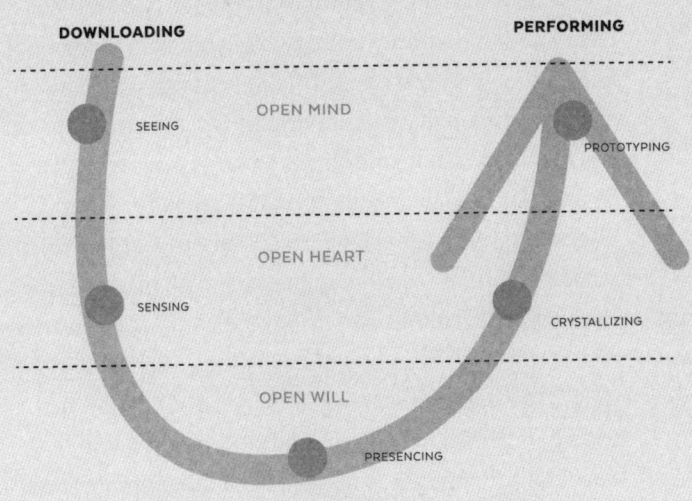

Figure 7. The U process: going from seeing the problem to seeing the solution

Theory U consists of three levels and seven stages. These seven stages are:

1. *Downloading.* At this first stage, our point of view is limited. When we're downloading, we're seeking confirmation of our own views and sticking to established patterns we can relate to our present situation. We use these familiar ways of thinking and acting to try to solve the problem as quickly as possible and immediately get to the final stage, *performing.* We need to let go of these habitual ways of thinking and acting in order to go through the u process. This is a prerequisite for learning as well. It means being open to Brilliant Failures, as Brilliant Failures by definition break patterns.

2. *Seeing.* The second stage is about being open to deviations from your expectations and postponing judgment. This requires opening your mind. This starts with recognizing and temporarily letting go of your own judgments, biased thoughts and ideas. This will change your way of seeing by broadening your perspective. It'll also help you see the added value of Brilliant Failures more easily.

3. *Sensing.* Dealing with complexity also requires learning how to deal with others, which is exactly what this third stage is about. It involves connecting with other people's thoughts and feelings and using that connection to arrive at a better understanding of each other. This understanding is the basis for seeking solutions and possibilities together. In dealing with Brilliant Failures, it's also very important for people to respect each other's ambitions, experiences and fears.

4. *Presencing.* This word is a blend of the words "presence" and "sensing." At this fourth stage, knowledge, feelings, intuitions and dreams come together. Past, present and future meet and the way ahead is seen. This is the level of

"open will" where you have no fear of the unknown, which means you're open to experiencing Brilliant Failures in the future. Here, at the bottom of the u, you access your source, the inner place from which you operate.

5. *Crystallizing.* At the fifth stage, the change is given shape and a vision of the ideas and future possibilities is created. This process is similar to the process of developing scenarios, which will be described in Chapter 7. Here, again, there's a clear link to dealing with Brilliant Failures, as the change process contains uncertainties. To reach your goal or realize your dream, you sometimes have to choose paths that lead through unfamiliar territory. Your visions of the future should therefore take into account the possibility that you might end up somewhere else or reach your goal in a different way. Serendipity plays an important role here as well. And this, too, has to do with "being open", including being open to deviations from your intended result or planned route to get there.

6. *Prototyping.* The sixth stage is about actually taking action. Based on shared insights and ambitions, future possibilities have been envisioned that will serve as a guide to change and point the way to the first steps. The motto here is "Failing Brilliantly in order to succeed as quickly as possible." This stage requires agility—moving, analyzing, adjusting course and moving again. The BriFa learning cycle is continuously repeated. At this stage, you also receive feedback on the ideas, observations and future possibilities that emerged in previous stages.

7. *Performing.* In this seventh and final stage, a new order and new patterns emerge. These are necessary for functioning and making the change effective. However, the validity of these new patterns must be reflected upon to prevent the new, initially desired situation from becoming a static and unsustainable model for the envisioned future.

Theory U describes a positive journey from the present to the future by seeking and finding enrichment of your own and other people's inner motivations and experiences. This process will only have a chance of success if you are open to the limitations of current patterns and to the opportunities presented by the new situation. But you must also be open to the possibility that things might go differently than expected, which means that sometimes you'll have to overcome fear, judgments, prejudices and cynicism. Fear is a primal response, and reducing fear is a central theme in thinking about Brilliant Failures. After all, this is about taking away the fear of the unknown, the fear of experimenting. The fear of talking about things that didn't go as hoped or expected, though, interferes with accepting and learning from the unexpected.

To overcome such obstacles you shouldn't be afraid, but rather "open" in your way of thinking and acting. This is related to the three levels of "open," as shown in Figure 7:

A. *Open mind.* Judgment limits your thinking and your ability to gain insight. A curious attitude helps you overcome prejudice and shows interest in the others involved. This level involves asking open questions, such as "What do you think of this?", "What am I trying to achieve here?", "Why do we always do things the same way?" and "What would happen if...?" An open mind goes beyond "good" and "evil" and other binary oppositions, searches for the facts, and takes a broad perspective.

B. *Open heart.* When your heart is open, you let yourself and others into your capital-S Self and your future. You're able to connect wisdom and to begin to experience the change process with complete trust.

C. *Open will.* At this level, it's important to truly want to change things. Fear is often greatest at this level. But if the will is truly there, you'll perceive risks differently. You'll see them, but your level of acceptance will be different. You'll also accept Brilliant Failures more readily. After all, your intentions were good and you acted with an open mind, while fully connected with your own and other people's wisdom and ambitions. You fully accepted the complexity of existence and the change and, in all this complexity, demonstrated the will to navigate to the future.

Applying Chapter 2

1. Think back to the last failure you were to some extent responsible for. Which of the Dirty Dozen factors can you identify in your own behavior?
2. Which area of life would you like to experiment and learn more about? What should you change to achieve this?

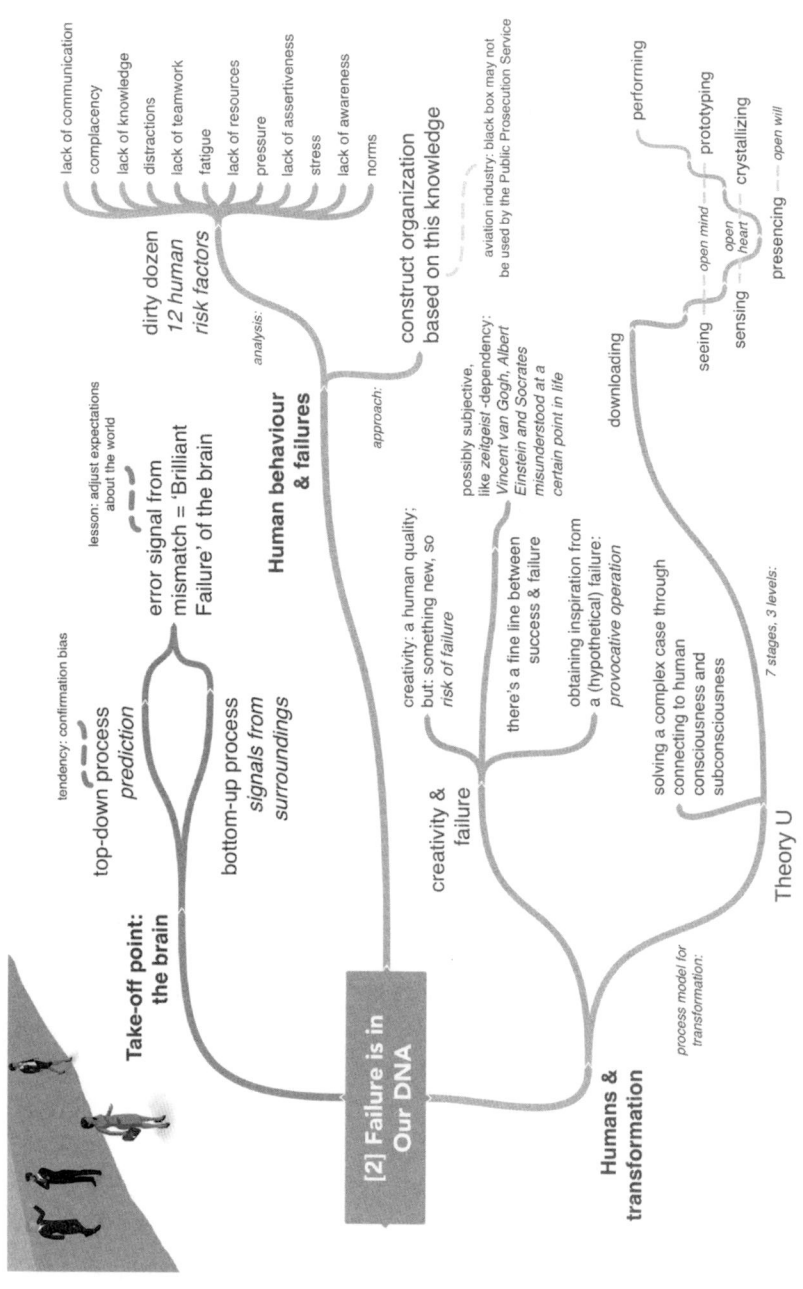

lack of communication
complacency
lack of knowledge
distractions
lack of teamwork
fatigue
lack of resources
pressure
lack of assertiveness
stress
lack of awareness
norms

dirty dozen
*12 human
risk factors*

analysis:

construct organization
based on this knowledge

aviation industry: black box may not
be used by the Public Prosecution Service

**Human behaviour
& failures**

approach:

performing

prototyping

crystallizing

open mind

*open
heart*

open will

seeing

sensing

presencing

downloading

possibly subjective,
like *zeitgeist* -dependency;
*Vincent van Gogh, Albert
Einstein and Socrates
misunderstood at a
certain point in life*

tendency: confirmation bias

lesson: adjust expectations
about the world

top-down process
prediction

error signal from
mismatch = 'Brilliant
Failure' of the brain

bottom-up process
*signals from
surroundings*

**Take-off point:
the brain**

creativity: a human quality;
but: something new, so
risk of failure

there's a fine line between
success & failure

obtaining inspiration from
a (hypothetical) failure:
provocative operation

creativity &
failure

solving a complex case through
connecting to human
consciousness and
subconsciousness

7 stages, 3 levels:

Theory U

**[2] Failure is in
Our DNA**

**Humans &
transformation**

*process model for
transformation:*

50

3. COMPLEXITY AS A CAUSE OF FAILING BRILLIANTLY

The world in which we live is changing ever more rapidly and its complexity is increasing. Major shifts are taking place in many areas of life, ranging from the rise of new economic and political superpowers to climate change and technological advances. At the same time, our globally connected world is getting smaller and smaller, mainly because of the Internet. Old barriers such as time, distance and money are disappearing, allowing everyone to exchange ideas and compete with each other at the same time and in the same place. It's getting considerably busier in the global markets of knowledge, ideas and services, where we increasingly have to earn our living. Mediocrity—directly related to fear of failure—just won't cut it in this world. This idea isn't new, by the way. In a nutshell, the importance of having an open attitude toward risk taking, experimenting, daring to fail and learning from failure has increased dramatically.

But what exactly is the difference between "complex" and "complicated," and why does it matter?

Complicated Systems

A system is complicated when its behavior is difficult but not impossible to predict based on the information you have. Take, for example, a car or a mechanical watch. Such objects look impressively complicated when you take them apart. Once you understand the function of each part, though, you will understand how the car or the watch works and be able to predict how it will behave. Or take difficult math problems: They may be complicated, but can often be solved with the right knowledge and skills.

Although we tend to assume that all mathematical problems can be solved, this isn't necessarily the case, as shown by Kurt Gödel's so-called incompleteness theorem. According to Gödel, an infinite number of mathematical statements can be made that can't be proven either true or false. His work meant a Brilliant Failure for others. Many had tried to prove that mathematics *is* complete, and that everything *can* be proven either true or false. This seemed so self-evident that mathematicians devoted their entire careers to this challenge. Their efforts were in vain, as it turns out, because Gödel's creative and ingenious article showed that not everything in mathematics can necessarily be proven true or false. Because this is such a highly complicated subject, even the best mathematicians encountered a Brilliant Failure here.

This is also an example of people spending much time searching in vain for certainty, being insufficiently open to the possibility that this certainty might not exist. We'll revisit this attitude in our discussion of Brilliant Failure archetypes, especially the Canyon archetype, in which people are insufficiently open to possibilities beyond their own thinking.

Complex Systems

Complex systems are fundamentally different from complicated systems. Just like a complicated system, a complex system consists of parts—components—that influence each other. The behavior of a complex system is the result of all interactions between its components and differs from that of a complicated system in an important way: It can't be predicted based on the properties of the individual components. People used to think that the unpredictable nature of complex systems, such as the weather, was caused by a lack of information. Adding the missing information would turn it into in a complicated system whose properties and development can be calculated using a computer if necessary. This turned out not to be true. Even if you know everything about a complex system, its behavior and development can still be unpredictable. However, it is true that if you're missing part of the information of a complicated system, it'll manifest itself to you as a complex system with the inherent uncertainty thereof.

Emergence

Properties that emerge at the system level cannot always be directly explained by the local, individual behavior of the components of the system and their mutual interactions. This concept is called "emergence."

Brilliant Failures can often be considered emergent phenomena. They're "hidden" in the system, as it were, and then suddenly show up. Emergent properties of the whole system are more than the sum of its individual parts and their local interactions. They're properties that can only exist in the collective; that is, they can't emerge through the addition of individual properties. The classic example is a flock of birds. Research has shown that flocking birds generally only look to their nearest neighbors to make sure they neither get too close nor stray too far. The collective behavior of a flock of birds, though, cannot be predicted based on these simple, local rules. In the case of emergence, the influence of local changes on collective behavior cannot be predicted. Sometimes a change has no consequences and sometimes a small change greatly affects the whole system. This gave rise to the popular myth of the butterfly flapping its wings and causing a storm on another continent. Incidentally, this admittedly appealing myth has been proven false, although small perturbations may indeed have a strong, seemingly random influence on the weather.

The previous chapter showed that people prefer to extrapolate in their attempts to understand and predict the world. They extend the application of a past development to the future in order to establish a direct connection between cause and effect. But such a connection doesn't always exist in our complex world, in which non-linear behavior and unpredictability go hand in hand. The more complex the world becomes,the greater the chance that things won't go according to plan—and the greater the chance that expectations will not be met. Failure will be lurking around the corner...

Of course, this doesn't mean that we should just stop making plans altogether. It does, however, mean that we should change our ways of thinking about planning and of dealing with unexpected results.

A good example of this behavior can be found in so-called fractals, which arise from relatively simple rules between adjacent components. The resulting structures can be very complex (and sometimes very beautiful) and may contain repeating patterns. This phenomenon is known as "self-similarity."

Figure 8. Example of a fractal

We regularly encounter patterns at different scales, such as the repeating patterns in fractals, in the world around us. Think, for example, of a coastline. As you zoom in to a smaller scale, you increasingly encounter more new structures that make the length of the coastline seem longer and longer. The coastline consequently appears to have a dimension greater than one, which you'd expect from a measure of length. Depending on the shape, the effective dimension can be any number between one and two, hence the term "fractal."

We run into fractal phenomena in everyday life as well: As we delve deeper into a subject or a problem, we see more and more issues to be aware of. If we remain at too superficial a level, we won't see these issues and run the risk of making wrong decisions based on an incomplete view of the situation. If, however, we delve too deeply into all the side issues, we'll lose sight of the overall picture. Later in this book we'll link failures resulting from either too superficial or too detailed a view to the Einstein Point archetype, inspired by the following quote from Albert Einstein: "Everything should be made as simple as possible, but not simpler." Or, as philosopher Friedrich Nietszche put it in his book *The Gay Science*:

Do not stay in the field!
Nor climb out of sight.
The best view of the world
Is from a medium height.

FRIEDRICH NIETZSCHE

There's another tongue-in-cheek way of illustrating that a system can best be managed by carrying out the analysis at the most appropriate level. There's a distance at which a person is optimally attractive to someone else. From up close you can only see the details, such as pimples and other irregularities, whereas from a great distance too little can be seen for attraction to take place. The perfect distance is somewhere in between.

In natural complex systems, higher-level rules are consistent with lower-level rules. The lower-level rules determine individual behavior as in the example of the flocking birds. As this should also apply to organizations and society, it's an interesting angle from which to view tension in top-down organizations. These kinds of organizations sometimes establish or assume rules at the organizational level that are inconsistent with what's happening at lower levels of the organization, which is something an organization with a bottom-up organizational structure would never do. Not taking lower-level rules into account can cause things to go wrong at higher levels.

Exceptions—that is, situations with a low probability of occurrence—occur in many systems. Far from the mean, the probability of a certain value occurring is rather low. Take life expectancy, for example. If the average life expectancy is eighty years, the number of people who die at either a much older or a much younger age decreases rapidly as you move away from the average. True outliers, e.g. people who live to or beyond the age of one hundred, have very little influence on the statistics and can be excluded from analysis in many cases. The formula for the normal distribution is as follows:

$$f(x) = \frac{1}{\sigma\sqrt{2\pi}}\, e^{-\frac{1}{2}\left(\frac{x-\mu}{\sigma}\right)^2}$$

In this formula, μ denotes the so-called expected value and σ denotes the standard deviation. The following image shows the well-known "bell curve."

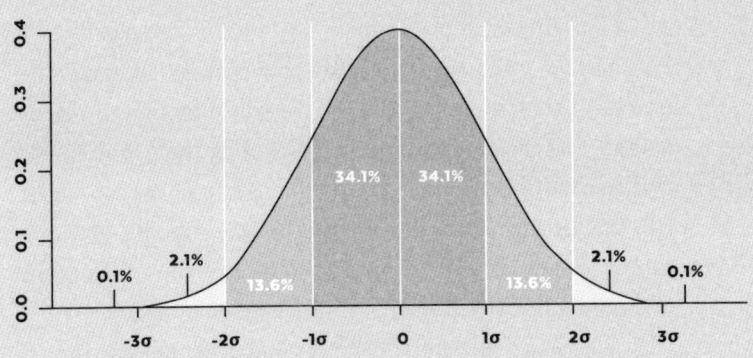

Figure 9. The bell curve of a normal distribution

As you move away from the average, the probability of the situation occurring decreases exponentially. This is why the contribution of the "tail" of the normal distribution to the behavior of the system is usually small.

There are, however, systems with "fat tails," in which occurrences far from the average do matter very much. In fact, complex systems regularly exhibit this behavior. It's also a manifestation of non-linear behavior, in which small effects may have significant consequences. In a fat-tailed distribution, probabilities far from the mean don't decrease exponentially, but via a power series:

$$f_X(x) \sim x^{-(1+\alpha)} \text{ as } x \to \infty, \qquad \alpha > 0.$$

Although the probability of occurrence does drop to 0 far from the mean, it does so much less rapidly than it does in an exponentially decreasing function. The contribution of outliers in fat-tailed distributions may thus carry much more weight compared to outliers in normal distributions.

The failure to prevent the Ebola outbreak

An interesting example of the importance of complexity thinking and the influence of a fat tail concerns the spread of diseases. A better understanding of the way infectious diseases spread is of great importance in combating them. The spread of a disease depends not only on the nature of the pathogen (the bacteria or virus), but also on the way people and their environments behave. Important factors here are the nature and number of interpersonal contacts people have.

If on average each person infects one other person, the outbreak won't spread; after all, there will only be one person who contracted the disease from me by the time I've recovered or died. But if on average each person infects more than one other person, because of their behavior and the nature of the pathogen, the disease may spread. The number of people one person infects on average is called the basic reproduction number. Figure 9 shows the reproduction numbers of several well-known infectious diseases.

Disease	Reproduction number
Measles and whooping cough	5-18
Chicken pox	7-12
Polio	5-7
Smallpox	1.5 – 20+
Seasonal flu	1.1 – 1.5
Ebola	1.1 – 3

Reproduction numbers of several infectious diseases. The numbers vary, not just according to the specific mutation of the pathogen but also according to the environment in which the disease occurs. (source: Sam Scarpino, www.youtube.com/watch?v=GC8ISx5jpXE)

The intention

In 2014 an Ebola epidemic struck West Africa. Although the reproduction number of this disease isn't very large (see Figure 9), it's still larger than 1, allowing it to spread. The World Health Organization has been severely criticized for its response during the Ebola crisis. Were the necessary precautions taken on time?

The approach
The precautions taken, such as information dissemination, were aimed primarily at the large group of people who have contact with a limited number of people, e.g. within families.

The result
But this was not enough. As it turned out, the ones who contributed significantly to the spread of Ebola were actually the outliers: The small group of people with a large number of contacts, especially health professionals such as doctors, nurses and paramedics. The crisis ended up claiming an exceptionally large number of lives among healthcare workers.

The lessons learned
The Ebola outbreak would probably have been less devastating if people had acted earlier. For example, doctors and nurses who had recovered and could no longer contract or spread the disease should have been allowed to return to work sooner. But they weren't, because people were assuming a normal distribution, insufficiently taking into account the complexity of the issue and the fat-tailed distributions associated with complex systems.

Complex Adaptive Systems
A major category of complex systems is the category of Complex Adaptive Systems (CAS). In these systems, the interactions between the components change over time. These changes depend on the condition of the system and are governed by a number of rules. The way the system develops, in other words, depends on the condition of the system at that point in time. This is also how "learning systems" arise, by adapting based on their history. Patterns emerge and are confirmed by the rules or disappear again.

This is why studying the patterns of a system can help you better understand it. The emergence, confirmation, disappearance and/or reemergence of patterns determine the dynamic nature of the system in question.

Examples of Complex Adaptive Systems are all around us. First and foremost, the brain is a CAS. We learn from our experiences, which enables us to make different decisionsthan we did before the moment of learning. Financial markets, such as stock markets, are complex and adaptive as well. The behavior of buyers and sellers dynamically determines stock prices; at a meta level, econometric models attempt to predict stock price developments by analyzing both stock market developments and current factors that may influence these developments in the future, such as macroeconomic prospects or phenomena of crowd psychology. Another example of a CAS is nature itself, including ecosystems. Evolution is based on a process of trial and error, in which it gradually becomes clear which changes (mutations) can survive and be sustainably integrated into the system.

Learning from failure is an important mechanism that leads to Complex Adaptive Systems. Taking away the incentive to learn limits our adaptive capacity and chances of future success.

Our World Has Truly Become Much More Complex
The world is in the middle of a perfect storm, with several important issues simultaneously at play. This can be compared to the specific circumstances in which natural phenomena arise. Tornadoes, for example, only form under particular temperature and pressure distribution conditions. We're living in an increasingly complex world in which major economic, technological and social changes are taking place. This is why we have to learn to deal with complexity and dynamism, which means we should be able to:
- deal with uncertainty;
- deal with change;
- deal with others.

Continuous technological advances have resulted in almost dizzying dynamic changes. Disruptive changes often come from outside an environment, rather than from within. The taxi industry wasn't disrupted by another cab company, but by an online platform: Uber. Airbnb became a major player in the hotel industry without owning any hotels. Banks no longer look to each other, but to tech companies such as Google, FinTech start-ups, crowdfunding platforms, etc. Former computer companies are now developing phones. In short, we're discovering that the world is larger and more complex than the limited environment in which we used to work and compete. The dynamism of such a system requires competencies such as mental agility and a learning mentality. It requires us to live "on the edge of chaos," to quote Stuart Kauffman (1991, 1995).

The inability of a person, organization or society to adapt to technological change may result in considerable failures. Examples include some major failed IT projects, or projects that failed because the necessary technology couldn't be developed or wasn't developed on time. But problems may also arisein the interface between people, society and technology. Some people may lose their way in the technological world and become unable to perform their daily tasks and activities because of their inability to deal with new systems.

Specific examples here are the increasing digitization, automation, robotization, and other forms of technological development. Some people welcome these new developments and see a future full of possibilities. But to many others our civilization is becoming more and more abstract and incomprehensible. We entrust computers with our lives, and we'll just have to trust that the rapidly increasing productivity and artificial intelligence will bring us wealth and well-being. There's a significant chance that many of our investments in technology won't produce the desired results at all if we don't make the necessary adjustments to the way we interact and work together. We should not only pay attention to technological innovation, but also invest in social innovation, as also shown by the Erasmus Competition and Innovation Monitor, one of the largest cross-industry surveys in the Netherlands covering various types of innovation (2015).

NT + OO = EOO

NEW TECHNOLOGY IN OLD ORGANIZATIONS RESULTS IN EXPENSIVE OLD ORGANIZATIONS

This is not to say that the aforementioned developments are negative or undesirable. On the contrary, they've led to spectacular growth of wealth and of well-being in many ways, such as better health, more educational opportunities, and other forms of personal and social value creation. However, none of it has got any simpler.

By the way, the term "artificial intelligence" is actually rather odd—there's nothing artificial about intelligence. It'd be better to speak of "additional intelligence" or "augmented intelligence" to indicate that we, combined with our own intellectual capacity, can achieve more than before. That's a much more positive way to frame this development!

Complexity in Projects and Programs

Many activities are structured and carried out in the form of projects. At the beginning of a project, we look ahead and form ideas and assumptions about the future. This means that a greater or lesser degree of uncertainty is involved. The risks of the project depend on its complexity, the degree of innovation, the commitment of those involved, and so on. We develop project plans to indicate what we're trying to achieve, what we'll need in order to achieve our goals, what risks have been identified and how we're planning to deal with these risks. Of course, it helps to take into account unexpected events as much as possible, but the fact remains that unexpected things can always happen.

In theory there's no difference between theory and practice, but in practice there is a difference between practice and theory.

Failure or partial failure of the project is possible. There are various ways to manage the risks. It's important to try to use as much knowledge as possible at crucial decision-making moments, including knowledge that was acquired in earlier projects (the double-loop learning process).

There are various moments before, during, and after a project in which knowledge is produced and applied. Sometimes this process is so dynamic and unpredictable that it's better not to plan the entire project, but to divide it into subprojects based on the learning processes and to let the next phase depend on the outcomes of the learning processes. This iterative form of project management is called "agile." Various tools have been developed for agile project management, such as scrum.

Teams use scrum to work toward results in an effective and flexible way. Although scrum is often used in the IT world, it's gaining traction in other industries as well. The goal of scrum is to increase the effectiveness of a project team by completing part of the work in a so-called sprint, reviewing the work together, and then using everyone's ideas and experiences to decide on the next sprint. In this way, the team learns as quickly as possible, experience is directly applied, and results are obtained more quickly. The customer should, however, take into account that the exact outcome of the project cannot be determined in advance. Each next phase of the project is determined on the basis of the intermediate result and the vision or mission of the project.

The term "scrum" comes from rugby, where it's a means of restarting play in which the players face each other, huddled closely together. The comparison was once made because of the way a rugby team tries to reach its opponent's goal line as a group. This requires cooperation, adaptability, speed, and self-organization—all elements that are of equally crucial importance to the multidisciplinary teams in agile projects.

But non-agile project management also involves frequent reflections and project members having to make decisions for the next phase of their project. In this, it's crucial to learn from and act on things that didn't go as planned. This applies to everyone involved, including the customer. It's not unusual for failure of a project to already be inevitable when the assignment is formulated.

Stopping can be a very important step in a project. Knowing when to stop is of great value. Continuing for too long results in wasted resources, frustrations, and an additional barrier to starting something new. Projects are often continued for too long. The reasons for this may vary, from unwillingness and ignorance to incompetence. The inability to stop, or stop at the right time, forms the basis of "the Junk," one of the Brilliant Failure archetypes that will be discussed in Chapter 5.

On the flip side, stopping too soon may mean wasting a great opportunity, although you often won't realize it. By using the knowledge acquired in the project and earlier learning experiences as much as possible, you'll become increasingly more adept at assessing which signs you should pay attention to in order to stop a project at just the right time.

Learning in and from projects and programs
Contribution by Theo van der Tak

Projects and programs, and projects and program management, are excellent vehicles for tackling new challenges. You can use projects and programs to achieve or pursue unknown and uncertain objects and situations in changeable environments. If the environment is stable and the product or service is clear and straightforward, it's much more efficient to follow routine. For example, all steps to issuing a passport have already been taken before and recorded in a manual, process description or algorithm. Fortunately, many organizational processes are like this, which helps save money on start-up costs. However, you won't get away with following routine if you have to, say, create a fraud-proof passport. A project would be the best way to go about this. It'd be a complicated project; you'd have to investigate matters such as biometrics, customs procedures, passport requirements of other countries, passport photo requirements, and so on.

The project would become even *more* difficult if you didn't just have to create a passport, but border control for all countries in the Schengen Area to reduce illegal immigration. This would be a complex challenge, with all kinds of factors at play whose cause-and-effect relationships are unclear. Nowadays, organizations tackle these kinds of situations in the form of programs. A program is about moving to a desired situation by initiating and implementing various kinds of projects, routines and processes. This often involves research, experiments and pilot studies. As opposed to a project, a program doesn't guarantee one result—a fraud-proof passport, in our example—but a different outcome: a situation with fewer illegal immigrants in the Schengen Area, possibly achieved by creating a fraud-proof passport, but also by developing all kinds of other instruments, procedures and international agreements. Depending on the effectiveness thereof, other instruments may also be developed based on previous experiences.

There must be room to learn from research, experiments and pilots in a program, more so than in a project. Project members learn to work together in a team to pursue one job with one result, often under time pressure and within a certain range of quality and costs. The scope of a program is wider. Program members learn to think about the relationship between the defined goal and the possible solutions that could contribute to this goal;effectiveness. If the program is limited in terms of manpower, budget or time, members also have to consider the quickest and/or cheapest solution: efficiency. Because the path to the goal isn't set in stone beforehand, they'll learn to creatively search for possible solutions together, giving them the opportunity to learn from those experiences and find even more solutions.

Both projects and programs involve dealing with stakeholders and risks—programs more so than projects, but the principle is the same. Another similarity is that learning occurs implicitly and is dependent on the team member's own initiative. Learning isn't the main focus of projects or even programs; the job is the main focus and requires a lot of dedicated energy from those involved. Because programs have a wider scope and longer duration, they provide more opportunity to devote attention to learning. Some programs have this as their goal, which makes it even clearer.

Learning from projects and programs
That's it for learning in projects and programs. But what about learning *from* projects and programs? Since the sixties, project management has become a common practice at which many people have become adept. You could say that much learning has taken place among many professionals. Over the years, sustainable changes have occurred in the way people, teams and organizations approach project management. The organizations that tackle these kinds of challenges should therefore be bursting with evaluations, reviews and audits about what can be learned from projects and programs. One example is the Dutch government's investigation into failed IT projects of the Elias Committee (see *Turn Failed IT Projects Into Brilliant Failures* in Chapter 5). Such evaluations essentially form a bridge between the world of projects and programs and the organizations in which projects and programs are used. Evaluations are often conducted in governments because they, as public and political organizations, must be held financially accountable.
If used correctly, evaluations can produce useful recommendations for making a next project or program successful. I deliberately use the words "if used correctly" here, because many evaluations don't have learning as their purpose.

They're often about identifying the person responsible to hold them accountable for going over the budget. But if any lessons are learned, they're about avoiding previously made mistakes in the future. This is why recommendations often come in the form of new rules and regulations, or involve developing organizational structures, additional checks, more training courses, certifications, and sometimes even changes in management or corporate culture.

Limited willingness to change
Another problem is the limited willingness to change among policy makers, such as members of the Dutch House of Representatives whose private interests get in the way. Even while the Elias Committee was presenting its findings, other members of the House were already calling for a new government IT project related to changing the national public transport payment system—within a year! Such unrealistic expectations of complicated and complex systems show an apparent lack of learning ability in politicians. In this kind of environment, the performance of projects and programs might not be able to improve much more.

Applying Chapter 3

1. Have you ever stopped a project or activity either too soon or too late? How did this happen? Which signs would you pay attention to in order to prevent this from happening again in the future?
2. Think back to the last time you did something that failed because it ultimately turned out to be more complicated than it initially appeared. What did you learn from this experience?

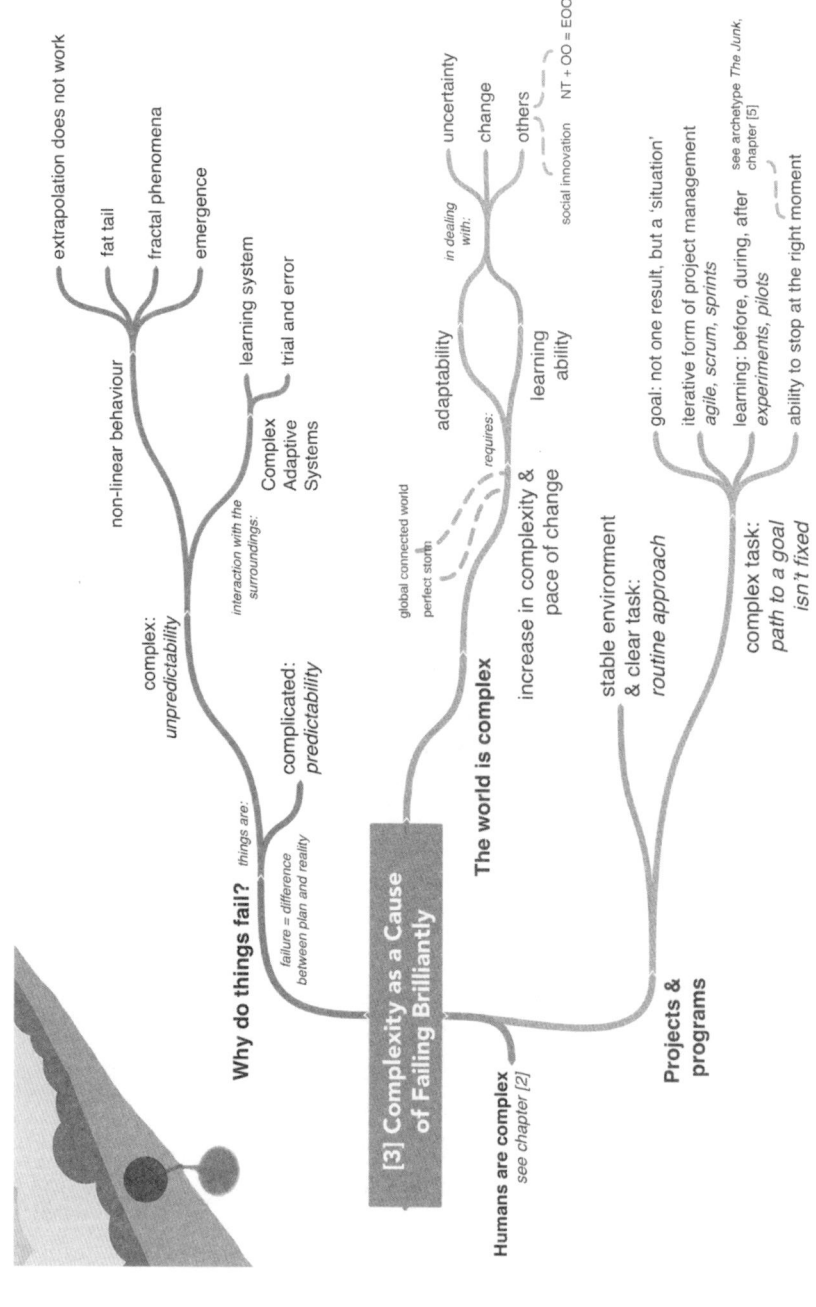

Why do things fail? *things are:*

- *failure = difference between plan and reality*

- complex: *unpredictability*
  - non-linear behaviour
    - extrapolation does not work
    - fat tail
    - fractal phenomena
    - emergence
  - *interaction with the surroundings:*
    - Complex Adaptive Systems
      - learning system
      - trial and error
- complicated: *predictability*

[3] Complexity as a Cause of Failing Brilliantly

The world is complex

- increase in complexity & pace of change
  - global connected world
  - perfect storm
  - *requires:*
    - adaptability
    - learning ability
    - *in dealing with:*
      - uncertainty
      - change
      - others
      - social innovation   NT + OO = EOO
      - *see archetype The Junk, chapter [5]*

Humans are complex
see chapter [2]

Projects & programs

- stable environment & clear task: *routine approach*
- complex task: *path to a goal isn't fixed*
  - goal: not one result, but a 'situation'
  - iterative form of project management *agile, scrum, sprints*
  - learning: before, during, after *experiments, pilots*
  - ability to stop at the right moment

4. A FAVORABLE CLIMATE FOR INNOVATION AND ENTREPRENEURSHIP

Innovation

"Innovation" comes from the Latin word *innovare*, which means "to reform" or "to change." Innovation is not just about new products and services. Every change implemented within or outside an organization that creates value can be considered an innovation. A useful framework for understanding this is the so-called Business Model Canvas (Figure 10), which represents the key elements of a business or business activity.

Figure 10. The Business Model Canvas, describing the different building blocks of a business or new proposition (Osterwalder and Pigneur (2010))

Innovation can occur in each building block or combination of building blocks of the business model. New revenue models, new partnership models, new employee-employer relationships (social innovation) etc. are just as much innovations as value proposition innovations (products and services). But, as the word "new" indicates, it hasn't been done before—which means you can expect surprises and can expect to go through the U process described in the previous chapter for each innovation.

Modular and architectural innovation

Innovations can be classified according to the degree of disruption and impact on the business model involved. Depending on the impact on the current state of affairs, innovation must be managed. We distinguish between innovations related to changes within the components of the system and innovations that change the composition of the components of the system. The former are modular innovations and the latter are architectural innovations (Henderson & Clark (1990), Baldwin & Clark (2000)).

Incremental innovations involve changes with little impact on either the components of the system or the links between the components, whereas radical innovations involve changes with great impact on both the components of the system and the links between the components. The four types of innovation are shown in Figure 11. It goes without saying that the probability of occurrence of a Brilliant Failure increases as the complexity and magnitude of the change increase.

"System" here refers primarily to the organization as a whole, but innovation may also occur in the building blocks of the business model. In any case, a system is a larger whole, whereas components may be stand-alone parts, such as the screen of a smart phone or a payment channel in banking services. A new type of screen and a redesigned payment channel are examples of modular innovations.

Examples of architectural innovations are the laptop and the introduction of online banking, which established new relationships between customers, channels and service providers.

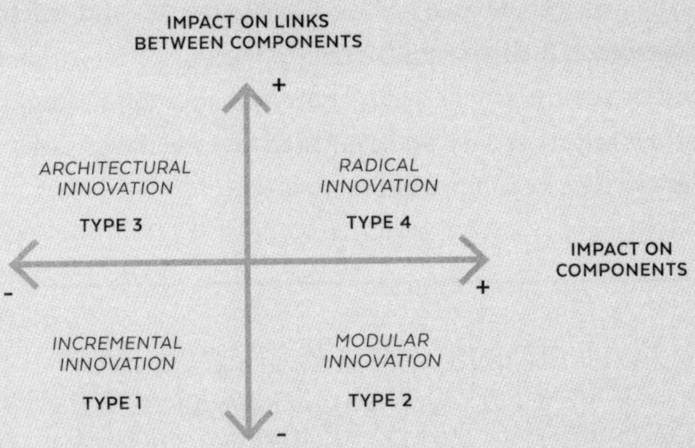

IMPACT ON LINKS
BETWEEN COMPONENTS

+

ARCHITECTURAL
INNOVATION

TYPE 3

RADICAL
INNOVATION

TYPE 4

IMPACT ON
COMPONENTS

−

+

INCREMENTAL
INNOVATION

TYPE 1

MODULAR
INNOVATION

TYPE 2

−

Figure 11. Henderson and Clark's four types of innovation

The Henderson-Clark model distinguishes four types of innovation. Type 1 and type 2 innovations occur within the existing model. Type 1 innovations involve adjustments within the current process that improve quality, margins, speed, customer satisfaction, etc., whereas type 2 innovations are intended to lead to new and improved products and services. Type 3 and 4 innovations involve fundamental changes to the business model (such as IBM's transition from product supplier to service provider) or even the development of entirely new business models (type 4). Examples of type 4 innovations are Apple's App Store and recent developments such as Uber, Airbnb and crowdfunding. A less recent example is Nokia's transition from a forestry and paper company to a telecommunications company based on the GSM standard, which had only just been developed and was entirely new at the time.

Innovation processes are increasingly often organized in an agile way, allowing for course adjustments to be made during and especially between the various phases of the process. This requires not the usual form of decision-making, in which all goals and milestones are determined in advance, but a form of decision-making in which new decisions can be made and resources can be reallocated based on intermediate results—through trial and error, in other words. It also means that accepting and learning from Brilliant Failures must be seen as an inherent part of any innovation strategy.

In my various roles, I've seen and evaluated many business cases. All my experiences can best be summarized as follows:

> *A business case is a collection of lies to make others decide what you want them to decide.*

Success has many failures
Contribution by Mathieu Weggeman

If you ask professionals in an organization to evaluate each other, it turns out that about 80 percent of professionals in the Netherlands consider each other to be good to excellent at their jobs. Other research has shown that people who are good at something first of all enjoy doing it and, second of all, would rather do something right than do something wrong. Based on these findings, managers can justifiably be recommended to give skilled professionals = approximately 80 percent of the population, space and trust when it comes to their process = the way they work, and only manage them in terms of output = the "what": what do I get from you at the end of the day? Freeing professionals from bureaucratic obligations such as keeping time logs, progress reports, project management reports and checklists allows their productivity to increase (even if it's only because they'll have more time for their primary task) and—perhaps even more importantly—their job satisfaction to increase as well.

Given space and trust, professionals will have more room for their second primary task: innovation. Knowledge is decaying at an increasing rate; new knowledge developed today may be outdated by tomorrow. But just keeping up with newly developed knowledge isn't enough to stay competitive in the long run. A knowledge-intensive organization must also make sure to sometimes be the first to launch new, innovative products or services. This benefits profitability, the image of the organization, and professional pride. There's no future without innovation, which is why innovation is the professional's second primary task. And most professionals, when given space and trust, will automatically start working on this task—especially if they're also given time to do so, as happens in organizations such as Canon, Google, IBM and Philips (casual Friday, free afternoons for research, etc.).

Allowing professionals to spend 10 to 20 percent of their time on innovation costs a lot of money, of course. On top of that, many innovation projects don't make it past the fuzzy front end.

During my time working at Philips's famous NatLab in the eighties, one of the research directors once said, "About one in ten of the innovation projects we're working on end up in a black box in our stores. But that one project pays for the nine other ones, and a lot more than that!" The general manager of Philips Research later mentioned this same ratio in his annual address, asking the researchers in the audience to only work on that one project from that moment on and abandon the other nine. He said this with a big smile, all too aware of the fact that you never know in advance which creative idea will eventually lead to a viable product and which Brilliant Failures you'll need in order to realize the market-changing potential of that one innovation or game changer.

To summarize: Allow professionals who are good at their jobs to innovate by giving them space and trust to do so, and realize in advance that not all of the resulting innovation projects will be successful—but a few of them will be. There's no success without failure!

Open Innovation: An Additional Layer of Complexity

Increasingly, the modern age requires us to work together. It starts at school, where students have to work on group projects. This can be quite a hassle, with one group member feeling like they're doing more work than the others, for example. But it's important to learn to work together at an early age, because you won't make it on your own. Collaboration is necessary—but it does introduce additional complexity, which isn't always easy. A collaboration may fail, and the entire project may fail along with it. Much research has been done on successful and failed collaborations. Summarizing the findings, it can be said that successful collaboration requires three types of fit. Firstly, there must be a cultural fit: a collaboration can only succeed if the people involved agree on a number of basic principles and values. Diversity is good, but it's very difficult and exhausting to work together if you disagree about literally everything. Secondly, there must be a strategic fit: although there is a common objective, each party always has ambitions of its own. A collaboration can only be successful if the common and individual objectives don't conflict with each other and, ideally, reinforce each other. Finally, there must be an operational fit: the parties should also be able to work together. Barriers to collaboration may include language barriers, incompatible (computer) systems, time differences, distances between locations, and time availability.

A failed collaboration is usually the result of a lack of fit in one or more of these factors, including lack of trust, commitment, results or changes in priorities..

Organizations are already aware of the fact that a more effective way to achieve innovation is generally not to develop all knowledge themselves, but to look for parties that already possess the necessary knowledge or are better able to develop it. The term for this, introduced by Henry Chesbrough (2003), is "open innovation." The logical opposite of open innovation is traditional, "closed innovation," in which parties develop and market their own ideas and knowledge.

It's essential to open innovation that an organization knows not only how to use its own knowledge, but also how to find and use relevant knowledge elsewhere. This means that a number of additional skills need to be developed: finding knowledge outside the organization, assessing this knowledge, and being able to connect it to the organization's existing knowledge. But it also requires the ability to connect with other parties and determine how the results of such a collaboration can be successfully brought to market. This in turn requires the organization to have a basic understanding of the knowledge possessed by the other party or parties, and to be prepared to share success—to believe that it's better to have a piece of a big pie than a small cupcake all to yourself. It could be said that, in addition to existing knowledge, a new skill has become relevant: interface management.

Supply chain complexity
Contribution by Frank Rozemeijer

When Boeing presented its highly innovative Dreamliner 787 in 2007, it promised to produce the jetliner for its customers in record time. To make this possible, drastic changes had been made to assemblage and supply chain management. Although the company had good intentions, it soon became clear that Boeing would not be able to deliver on its promise.

Production was beginning to slow down due to various minor disruptions in the supply chain. Some component suppliers were unable to supply altogether. At some point, there was even a shortage of simple fasteners such as screws, bolts and nuts, and Boeing had to turn to local hardware stores in order for production to continue. All these minor supply chain disruptions eventually resulted in a very considerable delay. The first Dreamliner was delivered in 2011, rather than in 2008 as promised.

Put simply, Boeing tried to change too many things in too little time. Launching a new and highly complex product before the supply chain was ready turned out to be a recipe for failure; solving the problems cost Boeing billions of dollars. This example shows that supply chain management is difficult and complex. Despite the good intentions of the parties involved (buyers, suppliers, sellers, customers), failure may lurk in various places, for example because of a lack of correct information, a lack of transparency in the supply chain, mutual distrust between parties, inability to cooperate internally, cultural differences between organizations, or contracts with wrong incentives.

Entrepreneurship Is a Process of Trial and Error

Although the word "enterprise" may refer to a business, one can be enterprising in many different areas of life—in love, on vacation, in sports, in academia, etc. We even use the term to describe children sometimes: "That's an enterprising kid!" This use of the term indicates that it's primarily about character and behavior, about exploring new opportunities and being active. The European Commission has adopted a definition of entrepreneurship that confirms it's about a certain type of behavior:

Entrepreneurship is an attitude that reflects an individual's motivation and capacity to identify an opportunity and to pursue it.

Importantly, enterprising people not only see opportunities, but also pursue them. When I'm watching a soccer game on TV, I see opportunities, but I don't act on them. This doesn't count as entrepreneurship. Based on the experience and input of many people I've talked with, the following behaviors and traits appear to be particularly characteristic of entrepreneurs:

- Passion, energy
- Taking risks, boldness
- Open and outward-oriented
- Flexible, adaptability
- Perseverance, stamina
- Pragmatic
- Result-oriented, focus
- Creative
- Exploring boundaries, questioning rules
- Networking, cooperating
- Smart, utilizing knowledge
- Eager to work

The fact that enterprising people deal with risks differently doesn't mean that they don't see danger, by the way; it just means that they try to assess the risks as accurately as possible to determine which risks they're able or willing to accept. Entrepreneurs do, however, tend to accept risks to a greater extent or attempt to address risks differently than less enterprising people.

Brilliantly bankrupt: A blessing or a curse?
Entrepreneurship, then, is about finding opportunities and creating value, for example through organizational changes or by introducing new products or services. In other words, there's a clear relationship between entrepreneurship and innovation. A characteristic aspect of this relationship is

that entrepreneurs who are developing new opportunities often don't possess the necessary means, but their passion and perseverance lead them to accepting the challenge and the inherent risks therein. Another inherent feature of entrepreneurship is failure.

Despite their willpower, one in two entrepreneurs is no longer active after five years, too often due to bankruptcy (Ondernemerschap.nl, 2011). Problems of succession may affect small- and medium-sized family businesses; in the case of second- and third-generation entrepreneurs, there are indications that less emphasis on innovation and being in the presence of the founder's shadow play a role (Bammens, Van Gils & Voordeckers, 2010).

Going bankrupt is not just a professional disappointment. It's a personal disaster for entrepreneurs and their loved ones, and a sometimes unnecessary loss of entrepreneurial spirit and innovation for the society as a whole. In the Netherlands, an estimated three billion euros are lost to corporate bankruptcy annually. Each year almost ten thousand companies are forced to close their doors, leaving behind tax debts and debts to banks and suppliers. Almost as many people a year appeal for personal debt restructuring, an estimated 25 percent of whom are entrepreneurs with one-man businesses. Estimates of bankruptcy-related job loss range from seventy thousand to more than a hundred thousand jobs a year. Including family members of bankrupt entrepreneurs, almost two hundred thousand people a year in the Netherlands are directly affected by the financial and personal consequences of corporate bankruptcy.

Bankruptcy seems to be a taboo subject: People it happens to would rather not talk about it, and people who see it happen in their environment are often equally hesitant to bring up the subject. This is particularly true in the case of family businesses or small- and medium-sized enterprises, where the owner/director is the face of the failed company. Entrepreneurship has been steadily on the rise in recent years; there are currently more than a hundred thousand new entrepreneurs in the Netherlands. The increase is greatest in the service sector and primarily due to the growing number of one-man businesses, which make up approximately 95 percent of new enterprises. Many people only temporarily engage in entrepreneurship: According to official figures provided by Statistics Netherlands (CBS), almost 50 percent of registered one-man businesses become inactive within five years.

The highest risk of bankruptcy is found in the corporate service sector, the construction industry, and the food and hospitality industry. When asked about the causes of their bankruptcy, entrepreneurs report financial problems, 70 percent; commercial issues, 70 percent; personnel issues, 58 percent; and clients going bankrupt, 55 percent. Liquidators, however, mention entrepreneurial incompetence, managerial problems, funding problems, and fraud, in that order. Robert Blom (2004) studied what entrepreneurs go through when they go bankrupt. He found that many are in financial trouble, almost a third have to sell their house, and family members are greatly affected by the situation in a quarter of cases. Nearly 15 percent get divorced or have relationship problems. A third of them find it difficult to get their lives back in order after bankruptcy, hindered as they are by misunderstanding, reproach and practical circumstances.

The Dutch Natural Persons Debt Restructuring Act came into force in 1998, taking away much of the year-long pain for one-man businesses that have gone belly up. Private and public limited liability companies in the Netherlands, however, are still covered by the Dutch Bankruptcy Act of 1893. Although various amendments have been made, the Act is still based on nineteenth-century rhetoric and not at all designed to meet the present needs of entrepreneurship. As Roel Nieuwenkamp, a high-ranking official of the Netherlands Ministry of Economic Affairs and Climate Policy, said in 2005, "Stigmatizing failed entrepreneurs is a typically Dutch trait."

In 2002, the Boston Consulting Group published a report appropriately entitled *Setting the Phoenix Free*, a study of the five hundred fastest-growing companies in Europe which showed that entrepreneurs who failed once learn from their mistakes and are more successful when they try again. Companies founded by entrepreneurs who were trying again turned out to grow faster in terms of revenue and number of employees than companies founded by entrepreneurs who hadn't previously failed. Presumably, this goes especially for people who Failed Brilliantly, i.e. who didn't make huge or avoidable mistakes, had good intentions, and learned from their failure. This is confirmed by research on the educational effects of bankruptcy conducted in 2001 by the ING Group Economics Department in collaboration with the Netherlands Ministry of Economic Affairs.

"Entrepreneurial renewal," to use the term coined by the Boston Consulting Group, also leads to GDP growth and more employment opportunities. In our discussion of Brilliant Failures, it's important to recognize the value of going bankrupt in a "brilliant" way, not due to fraud, intent, or culpable incompetence, and to give people who went brilliantly bankrupt another opportunity to realize their entrepreneurial aspirations. The 2006 publication, *Tweede Kans. Lessen in vallen en opstaan* [*Second Chance. Lessons in Trial and Error*], convincingly argues that sidelining bankrupt entrepreneurs results in great value loss.

The question is whether one's chances of success are greater the first or the second time. A person who starts another business shows perseverance and has more knowledge than they did the first time. This is an argument in favor of developing specific facilities for those who try entrepreneurship again after bankruptcy, such as second-chance credit or a second chance fund that only invests in companies headed by people who've previously gone brilliantly bankrupt.

In the United States, failing as an entrepreneur is considered more of a learning experience than a personal failure. Or, to quote Henry Ford, "Failure is simply the opportunity to begin again, this time more intelligently." After his Internet company Bitmagic flopped in the Netherlands, Michiel Frackers received various attractive offers from U.S. companies including becoming European Managing Director at Google, for example." I received zero offers from Dutch companies. In the U.S. they said, 'Good! Now you have a little blood on your nose.' Everyone says you learn more from your failures than your successes, which is my personal experience as well. But in the Netherlands we don't really seem to mean it," Frackers said. Of course, there's collateral damage sometimes, and it's sometimes too easy for entrepreneurs in the U.S. to pass the damage on to others and continue without problems. Let's put it this way: If the Americans would look to the Dutch and the Dutch would look to the Americans, they'd both be looking in the right direction.

New entrepreneurship: Start-ups and start-downs
We're all familiar with hotspots for new and innovative entrepreneurship such as Silicon Valley, where ideas, knowledge and capital meet. But the twenty-first century has seen the need for and interest in new entrepreneurship growth worldwide. Each year, two hundred companies that can be considered start-ups are founded in the Netherlands. Only one in ten

of these companies become internationally successful; the others remain small businesses or disappear within a few years, according to the 2015 statistics. There are various reasons why start-ups fail: They may not be innovative enough, they may run out of money, their team may not be good enough, they may be beaten by the competition, or their product or service may simply not be good enough. Was there no way for those 180 failed start-ups to know this in advance? Another important reason why an innovative development may fail is that it must ultimately be able to survive in a complex world. Something that works in a limited environment may be confronted with new circumstances and requirements in a wider environment, and fail to meet them. In terms of business development, it can be said that a successful start-up phase doesn't guarantee that the next phase—continued growth—will also be successful. There are essentially three distinct phases:

■ proof of concept;
■ proof of business;
■ proof of success.

During transitions between phases, it's important to carefully consider a number of aspects that will or should change at that point in time, such as the skills of the team (which may lead to changes in the team), type of customers or clients, type of financing, and the governance structure of the organization. Various Brilliant Failures can be explained by the inability to sustain a concept in an increasingly complex context, rendering initial success unsustainable. This is "the Bear's Skin," to use one of the terms that will be elaborated upon in our discussion of Brilliant Failure archetypes in Chapter 5: encountering problems during scale-up of something that worked as a prototype or experiment.

All self-respecting universities have so-called incubators, places where young, beginning entrepreneurs attempt to realize their plans and knowledge. They often receive support in the form of accommodations, advice, access to funding, exposure, and so on. There are also many courses aimed at developing the skills necessary for entrepreneurship. Almost always, however, exclusive attention is paid to the start-up phase, despite the fact that the vast majority of companies don't succeed at all. Oddly enough, entrepreneurship programs, incubators, Centers for Entrepreneurship, etc.

pay little to no attention to the most likely scenario of failure. What do you do when things start going south? How do you limit the damage? Maybe a plan B could be developed to create space for something new by terminating an activity. You'll also gain much new knowledge in the "start-down" phase. How can you use this knowledge to the fullest extent, the way you used the knowledge gained in the start-up phase? The answers to these questions may be very valuable, but they aren't addressed within the often opportunistic context of entrepreneurship programs.

It appears that the main cause of entrepreneurial failure is the product or service not meeting the needs of the market. Another major cause is running out of money. Developing something new often takes longer than anticipated, whether in terms of technical realization or market development. Incidentally, people in Europe are more inclined than people in the United States to "pull the plug" if not enough revenue or profit is generated within a certain period of time.

Even so-called gazelles, young and very fast-growing companies, don't always survive in the long run. "Gazelle" seems a somewhat strange term to use here; after all, gazelles are quiet, shy prey animals that exhibit herd behavior—not exactly what comes to mind when we think of successful entrepreneurs... In any case, recent research (Röskes (2017)) shows that Dutch gazelles do have a slightly better chance of survival than the average start-up. Almost half of the 269 gazelles surveyed are still growing steadily. A third of the companies that received Gazelle Awards from the Dutch Financial Times between 2006 and 2016 are still growing, though no longer at the explosive rate for which they were nominated at the time.

Whereas new companies primarily need the perseverance of individual entrepreneurs to turn failure into success, many hierarchical and results-driven companies need social innovations to create a culture that is accepting of entrepreneurship and the risks associated with it. As previously argued, this requires an appropriate organizational culture. Only then will destructive fear of failure in both entrepreneurs and employees make way for a responsible, yet entrepreneurial view of risk in relation to success—something from which we will all eventually benefit. Chapter 8 takes a closer look at the kinds of environments that allow for this.

F.A.I.L.: First Attempt In Learning for Start-Ups
Contribution by Bas Ruyssenaars

The website autopsy.io contains a long list of start-ups that didn't make it, including the reasons why—provided by the founders themselves. These reasons range from practical; "did not scale fast enough", and hilarious; "another casualty in the decline of Flash", to tragic and relatable; "stuck with the wrong strategy for too long." Your aim is to reach a particular goal, but getting there requires continuous course adjustments. This in turn requires cognitive flexibility, resilience, and the ability to see and capitalize on new opportunities. Whereas sticking to a preformulated strategy might've worked for companies two decades ago, continuous adjustments based on feedback from the market are necessary today. Fear is a poor adviser in this matter. Research has shown fear to be an important factor that prevents people from reflecting, taking some distance, and thinking in scenarios. Fear stifles innovation by narrowing your world down and making you cling to what you already know. This fear is often twofold: There's the fear of trying something that might fail, and there's the fear of talking about something that's going wrong or went wrong.

A practical example of entrepreneurs who aren't afraid to talk about their failure is HelloSpencer, a Dutch start-up delivery service. HelloSpencer aimed to deliver any order within sixty minutes. The service didn't make it. In September 2017, the founders announced that they couldn't get the business model for their anything-on-demand service to work. And then they did something unusual: They published their main failures and lessons, such as "dream big, start small," on their website. HelloSpencer hoped to grow organically by starting very small, with just a phone number for text delivery orders. Placing personal experiences between delivery people and customers, rather than the logistics process, at the heart of their business gave them much insight into customers' buying motives and made them feel like they were onto something big. Unfortunately, this also meant that they were too focused on daily logistics and didn't have a clear focus on time. Or take "hit your targets." Making a delivery service profitable is ultimately about volume. Although HelloSpencer was attracting more customers weekly, their growth phase was taking too long. They needed either more volume more quickly or funding for a longer period of time. A final lesson: "Keep everyone on board." Putting together a team with enough talent and energy is step one, but making sure everyone can continue to develop themselves—not just as a team, but also on a personal level—is at least as important in retaining people. By the way, if you're wondering what happened to the HelloSpencer guys: Half of them went to work for the Dutch SNS Bank and the other half tirelessly continued to pursue entrepreneurship with new or existing start-ups.

My own start-up adventure involves an innovative sports product and concept called YOU.FO. A sort of cross between ultimate Frisbee and racket sports or stick-and-ball games such as tennis and field hockey, YOU.FO involves throwing and catching an aerodynamic ring with specially designed sticks. If there's anything I've learned from this initiative in the last few years, it's that business strategies must be continuously adjusted based on market feedback. Having won various national and international awards, I assumed I would be able to bring YOU.FO to market with distribution partners, using a top-down approach. The reality turned out to be much more complex. This innovative game requires much more bottom-up marketing effort; people need to experience the game by playing it, and learn how to play it in order to stay enthusiastic about it. We're now working with a Germany-based sports consultancy club to set up a global community.

This is a completely different approach from the one I initially had in mind. And this business adventure is taking much longer than expected. In this respect, I'll take the lessons shared by HelloSpencer and others to heart!

Like autopsy.io, the Institute of Brilliant Failures aims to encourage learning—without shame—from start-ups that didn't make it right away. Sharing and learning from failure isn't just something that has to be done after the fact, by the way. It's especially relevant *during* a start-up process to periodically reflect on your own assumptions and approach and to share your reflections with others. In short: Sometimes you earn, sometimes you learn.

Applying Chapter 4

 1. To assess the climate for innovation in your organization, you can take the survey by scanning the QR code on the right or visiting https://nl.surveymonkey.com/r/InnovationEnvironment.

2. Have you ever undertaken an entrepreneurial venture that failed? Did you try again after that? Did you do better? If not, try again!

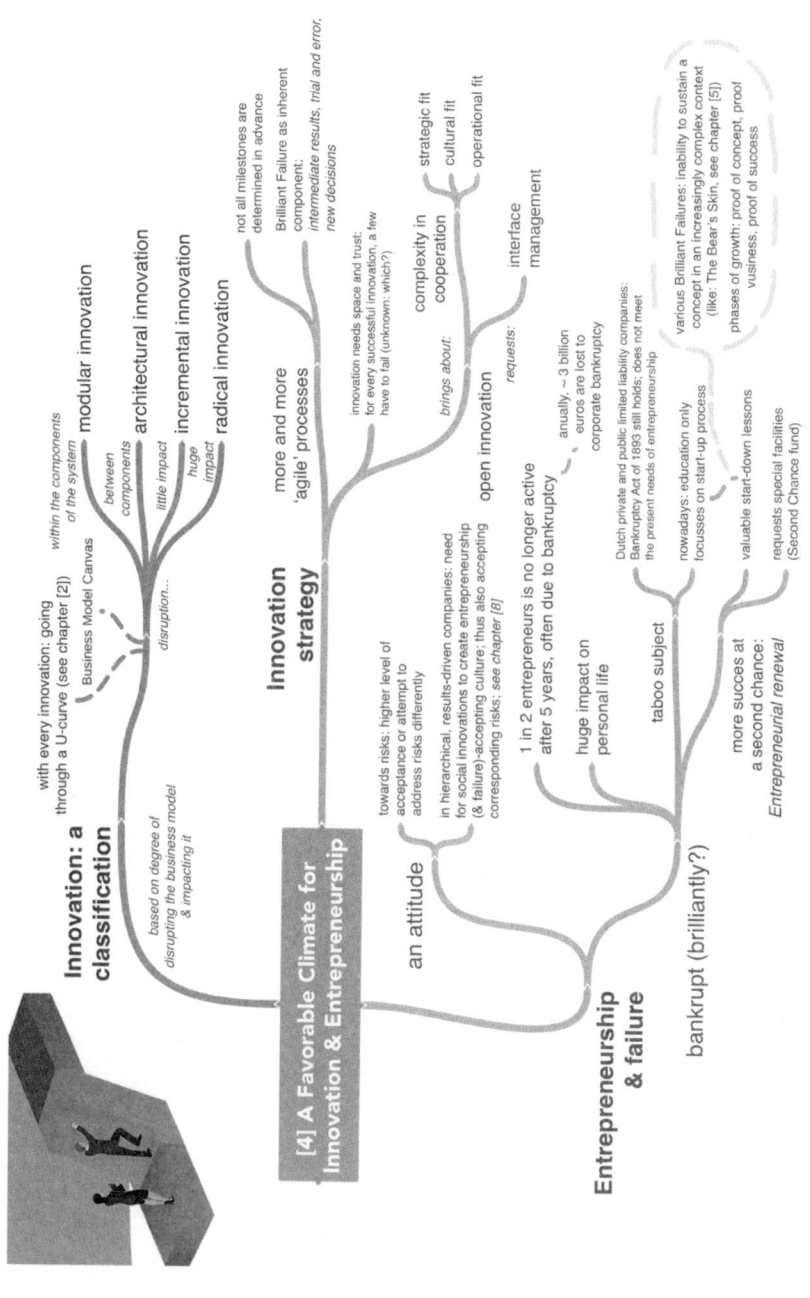

[4] A Favorable Climate for Innovation & Entrepreneurship

Innovation: a classification

based on degree of disrupting the business model & impacting it

with every innovation: going through a U-curve (see chapter [2]) — Business Model Canvas

disruption...

- within the components of the system → modular innovation
- between components → architectural innovation
- little impact → incremental innovation
- huge impact → radical innovation

Innovation strategy

more and more 'agile' processes

not all milestones are determined in advance

Brilliant Failure as inherent component: *intermediate results; trial and error, new decisions*

innovation needs space and trust: for every successful innovation, a few have to fail (unknown: which?)

open innovation

brings about: complexity in cooperation → strategic fit, cultural fit, operational fit

requests: interface management

an attitude

towards risks: higher level of acceptance or attempt to address risks differently

in hierarchical, results-driven companies: need for social innovations to create entrepreneurship (& failure)-accepting culture; thus also accepting corresponding risks; see chapter [8]

Entrepreneurship & failure

1 in 2 entrepreneurs is no longer active after 5 years, often due to bankruptcy

huge impact on personal life

taboo subject

bankrupt (brilliantly?)

anually, ~ 3 billion euros are lost to corporate bankruptcy

Dutch private and public limited liability companies: Bankruptcy Act of 1893 still holds; does not meet the present needs of entrepreneurship

nowadays: education only focusses on start-up process

valuable start-down lessons

requests special facilities (Second Chance fund)

more succes at a second chance: *Entrepreneurial renewal*

various Brilliant Failures: inability to sustain a concept in an increasingly complex context (like: The Bear's Skin, see chapter [5]) — phases of growth: proof of concept, proof of business, proof of success

5. A COMMON LANGUAGE: ARCHETYPES

Being open to the unexpected and learning from the unknown is a precondition for innovation and contemporary entrepreneurship. This is but one aspect of our plea for Brilliant Failures, though. Learning from each other in order to avoid the same pitfalls may be even more important. Our ultimate goal is a society focused on sharing knowledge. For successful transfer of knowledge to occur, it's very important to have a clear, common language that appeals to everyone's imagination. It was with this in mind that we introduced the BriFa method in Chapter 1, to which we'll now add an important element: Brilliant Failure archetypes. This approach is based on the human tendency toward pattern recognition. Over and over again we've observed in practice how valuable these archetypes are to knowledge sharing within companies and organizations.

The archetypes make Brilliant Failures more easily identifiable and transferable, providing a very sound basis for actually formulating and applying learning experiences. A major additional advantage is that people enjoy sharing their failures this way, and don't hesitate to talk about even their most painful failures. This allows others to learn from them as well.

Pattern Recognition

Pattern recognition and pattern processing are important aspects of intelligence. We think and learn by discovering, recognizing and classifying patterns in the world around us. This is because our brains have self-organizing, pattern-forming mechanisms. The brain consists of neurons that use electric signals that move from cell to cell. The brain isn't static, but dynamic and changeable. Neuroplasticity is the ability to form new connections between nerve cells, enabling us not only to learn new things, but also to change our habits and behavior. Neuroplasticity is a characteristic of the human neural system as a whole. When you successfully learn something new, a new set of connected neurons has been formed and become active.

You'll recognize a pattern more quickly if you observe it more consciously. We're constantly bombarded with information, much of which is filtered out by the brain. But there are certain situations in which certain patterns stand out more clearly, something to which we ourselves can contribute. A good example of this is the frequency illusion, also known as the Baader-Meinhof phenomenon. This term was coined by an Internet user who was unfamiliar with the Baader-Meinhof Group, a West German far-left militant organization, before stumbling upon the name twice within twenty-four hours. The phenomenon manifests itself in many different ways. After buying an exclusive car, for example, you'll suddenly notice other people driving the same model much more often than before. A friend of mine once complained to me about his car model being too popular. I said, "You should be glad, because that means it's a good car. Everyone wants it." He jokingly replied, "I want a car everyone wants, but no one can afford."

After hearing a song you enjoyed, you'll suddenly notice hearing it much more often. After deciding to book a vacation to Canada, you'll suddenly find out that many other people had the same idea. Your brain has been primed to notice these patterns, so you're quicker to pick them out from a wealth of information. Factors that influence this are how recently you received the information in question, how often you receive it, and what it means to you (your connection to the information).

Using archetypes is an interesting way of applying the Baader-Meinhof phenomenon as a means of encouraging pattern recognition.

As defined on Wikipedia, an archetype (from Ancient Greek αρχη, meaning "first" or "origin") is a "pure" or idealized basic form that is copied or emulated by later versions. Personifications, objects or concepts from cultural tradition such asliterature, mythology and religion, or even history like heroes can serve as archetypes.

The BriFa method was partly inspired by TRIZ©, a method used worldwide to classify and better understand innovations, but also as an instrument for generating innovations. TRIZ is a Russian acronym that stands for *Teoriya Resheniya Izobretatelskikh Zadatch* (теория решения изобретательских задач), which means "theory of inventive problem solving." The TRIZ method has a fascinating history. Shortly after the Second World War, the Russian inventor, Genrich Altshuller, started working in the patent department of the Soviet Navy. There, he not only continued his activities as an inventor but also studied a great number of patents held by others. He concluded that every invention could, in one way or another, be described as the removal of a technical contradiction. In Altshuller's view, innovation wasn't the result of chaos, luck and a mystical kind of inspiration, but something that could be systematically achieved by applying a number of principles.

Firmly convinced of the value of his work, Altshuller and his colleague Shapiro decided to send Joseph Stalin a letter stating that a methodological approach to innovation would be much more effective than the nation's current, chaotic approach. This criticism was seen as an attack on the nation and Altshuller was exiled to Siberia. His inventive ability helped him survive there. For example, he wasn't allowed to sleep, so he pasted circles of cigarette paper with black dots drawn on them onto his closed eyelids to make it look like he was awake. After Stalin's death, Altshuller returned, continued his work, and set up an institute where much research was done and many people were trained. This resulted in a worldwide TRIZ movement, making this method the standard for systematically and creatively solving complex problems. The original work by Altshuller and Shapiro (1956) is still the basis of the TRIZ method.

A simpler, stripped-down version of TRIZ was later developed by Israeli students: SIT, short for Systematic Inventive Thinking. This method consists of five basic principles that can be used to describe over 70 percent of all innovations, both product and service innovations. SIT is a very popular creativity technique in the business world.

Patterns in Failing Brilliantly: Sixteen Archetypes

Although the specific details and context are different for each Brilliant Failure, we've observed that the reasons why things go differently than expected are often similar. By analyzing a large number of cases, we've determined these causes of failure and subsequently developed sixteen archetypes to help you identify and learn from failures. The archetypes also have a classifying function; each case can be classified into one or more archetypes, allowing examples of similar Brilliant Failures to be found quickly and easily.

The archetypes further provide a good starting point for storytelling and sharing knowledge through stories. Practice has shown that these archetypes play a very important role in being able to analyze why things turned out differently than planned. These archetypes form the core of the BriFa method. The method involves recognizing the relevant archetypes, describing and making accessible learning experiences, and subsequently linking these learning experiences to new situations in which this knowledge may be relevant.

We'll first provide an overview of the sixteen Brilliant Failure archetypes.

1. *The Elephant* (the whole is greater than the sum of its parts)

Sometimes things only become clear when they're considered from various angles. The whole picture only emerges when observations from different perspectives are combined. We essentially project our observations, causing us to miss important information sometimes. If several of these "projections" are made, however, the original can be reconstructed. This phenomenon is well illustrated by the parable of the blindfolded men and the elephant. Six blindfolded men are asked to touch an elephant and describe what they're experiencing. One man feels a snake (trunk), another a wall (side), another a tree (leg), yet another a spear (tusk), the fifth a rope (tail), and the last one a fan (ear). None of the participants have described a part of an elephant, but when they share and combine their observations, the elephant "emerges." This, then, is an example of emergence: The elephant only exists in the shared complex world. Many phenomena are emergent in the sense that they're only fully visible when all perspectives are used.

Ford car model names

The intention
Automobile manufacturer Ford wants to give its car models appealing names. These names should be recognizable in the markets in which the cars are sold and be associated with the brand appearance and/or car model in question.

The approach
Lists of potential names are generated with the help of a marketing team and marketing agencies. A name that best fits the brand experience eventually comes out on top. Sometimes the name is changed to be more suitable for a specific market.

The result

Car model names usually do fit the car and the market in which the car is sold. But this isn't always the case. Ford in particular has a penchant for choosing ill-advised brand names, as illustrated by the following examples:

Ford Pinto (Portuguese: Ford Small Penis)
Ford Caliente (Mexican Spanish: Ford Street Whore)
Ford Fiera (Spanish: Ford Ugly Old Woman)
Ford Cortina (Spanish: Ford Old Jalopy)

The lessons learned

A car name is like an elephant: You'll have to consider the meaning of a word from all perspectives (languages) to make sure the name really is a suitable one.

And there's more...

In Ford's defense, we can list a few brand name failures by other car manufacturers: Fiat Croma (a frying and baking product in the Netherlands), Fiat Brio (a Dutch butter brand), Fiat Uno (French: Fiat Idiot), Toyota MR2 (French: Toyota Merde, Toyota Shit), Nissan S-Cargo (French: Nissan Snail), Mazda Laputa (Spanish: Mazda The Whore).

2. *The Black Swan* (unforeseen developments are part of the game)

Not everything can be foreseen, and unexpected developments can completely disrupt our plans and expectations. Shit happens! We can try to partly anticipate the unexpected by having a plan B in place, for example by setting aside some money in case an enterprise fails. We can also try to accept adversity and see if there's anything to be salvaged or learned from our setbacks. In any case, it's important to be aware of the fact that not everything can be planned to a "T" in our complex world. Uncontrollable events may occur in the system: you could start a company on September 11, 2001 and a new technological breakthrough could render your product redundant. You could write a thesis on cryptocurrencies and buy Bitcoins when they're still less than a dollar... Anything could happen. External circumstances can ruin your plans even when you haven't actually done anything wrong. Nassim Nicholas Taleb (2007) wrote *The Black Swan*, a remarkable book about unexpected developments that come as a surprise and end up having a major effect. He explains how important it is to realize that we don't know what we don't know, but that that which we can't know or couldn't have known could still be important. These kinds of unforeseen events are often emergent phenomena in our complex world.

Bankruptcy caused by Russian import ban
www.boerenbusiness.nl/artikel/10862922/importban-rus-land-treft-niet-alleen-varkenshouder

Dutch meat processing company Beusmeat used to produce and export two to three hundred pig heads a week for the Russian market. Because of the 2014 Russian import ban on EU products, the company lost its main sales market and ran into trouble. Its general manager, Paul Wellink, tried in vain to turn the tide by announcing two rounds of redundancies; eighty flexible-contract jobs were cut in February 2014 and a hundred and twenty temp jobs were cut in October 2014. Beusmeat held various rounds of redundancies in 2014. Why did the company ultimately fail to make it? According to Wellink, "Beusmeat's termination of business activities is the result of the closing of the Russian market and the ensuing economic consequences. This isn't the first time in the last ten years that the Russian market has been closed for political reasons. In the past, however, these situations were often short-lived. It's not just the Russian market; the company hasn't developed satisfactorily in other market segments either. As a result, volume has decreased significantly and we've suffered heavy losses. Of course, we tried to compensate for the loss of the Russian market and found other market opportunities. Unfortunately, these alternative sales markets insufficiently compensated for the lost Russian market. We currently don't see any opportunities to restart the company."

3. *The Wrong Wallet* (one person's advantage is another person's disadvantage)

In complex situations it can be difficult to predict the specific advantages and disadvantages of a project, including who the disadvantaged will be. It frequently happens that a change is positive for the system as a whole (cost savings, better service, improved public health...), but occurs at the expense of one or more parties within the system. Another example is a situation in which environmental improvements occur at the expense of employment opportunities or vice versa. Such dilemmas regularly cause solid value cases—which create value in terms of financial, social or natural capital—to fail due to a negative effect at a local level. The one who invests is not the one who profits. These kinds of Brilliant Failures may be difficult to prevent because they require systems thinking: Other players will have to figure out how those who may be negatively affected can be persuaded to contribute anyway. If it's about money, compensation provided by the collective is sometimes necessary in order to create an acceptable win-win situation or at least not alose not-lose situation in which one person's wallet doesn't benefit at the expense of someone else's.

The Swedish six-hour working day

The intention
The Swedish government wanted to study the effects of a six-hour working day. The question was whether a shorter working day would lead to improved well-being, higher productivity and better service. The concept had already been tested a few times, for example at the Swedish Toyota factory and IT company Filimundus. The underlying idea is Parkinson's Law (1955), which states that the amount of time someone needs to perform a task increases as the amount of time available for the task increases.

The approach
In an elderly care facility in Gothenburg, Sweden, 68 nurses only had to work six hours a day while receiving full pay.

The result
Initial results were positive. Employees felt healthier and took fewer sick days. Clients experienced improved service. However, Parkinson's Law doesn't apply to these kinds of environments: The work couldn't be done in six hours, as a result of which seventeen additional nurses had to be hired. This cost almost two and a half million euros over two years. In other words, the improvements in employees' health and wellbeing and the better service for clients were financed with money from the wallet of the facility's management. The experiment failed.

The lessons learned
If it's clear that there is a party that will be negatively affected by a project, this party must be given a higher-level incentive to participate anyway. In this case, it was known in

advance that there would be additional costs to be paid for by the employer. Either the staff should have been paid less or the facility's income should have increased.

The work environment didn't help either: Scandinavians on average don't work themselves to the bone in the first place, with only one percent of employees logging more than 50 hours a week.

4. *The Bridge of Choluteca* (problems don't stay in one place)

The world is not only complex, but also very dynamic and therefore changeable. Sometimes we try to solve a problem, but as soon as we've succeeded the problem turns out to have moved elsewhere or a new problem arises—the Law of Conservation of Misery, if you will. It can also happen that there are several risks involved, and that addressing one risk can't prevent another problem from popping up. This often applies to dealing with people as well: As you're trying to meet their wishes, they keep conjuring up other wishes or demands. It's like playing whack-a-mole.

An interesting example of a problem that unexpectedly moved is a bridge in Honduras. Choluteca Bridge was built in the thirties by the U.S. Army Corps of Engineers. It was designed and built to withstand even the worst hurricanes.

Figure 12. Choluteca Bridge: Useful in the past, but not anymore

The bridge indeed proved to be of exceptional quality when Hurricane Mitch struck the area in 1998. Although the hurricane caused extensive damage, Choluteca Bridge was undamaged. Unfortunately, floodwaters receded to reveal that the course of Choluteca River had moved several hundred feet. The bridge no longer spanned the river, but the dry land beside it.

The lesson here is that research and solutions were entirely correct at the moment when the project began, but the changing and moving of the problem can ultimately render the result useless.

The Fuel Cell boat that couldn't refuel

The intention
The first hydrogen fuel cell-powered tour boat was to change the face of the Amsterdam canals forever. It was a pioneering idea: a noiseless canal boat that didn't produce harmful emissions, didn't stink, and didn't use fossil fuels.

The approach

In late 2006/early 2007 a consortium of Dutch companies, Fuel Cell Boat BV, agreed to develop and build a hydrogen-powered boat. The 72-foot hydrogen vessel was to be used as a canal cruise boat in Amsterdam.

Nemo H2 was ceremonially launched by former Alderwoman Marijke Vos in 2009. The boat made a brief appearance at maritime event SAIL Amsterdam 2010 and was nominated for Ship of the Year 2011. Shell Amsterdam planned to have its employees use the boat on their daily commute to its building on the other side of the river IJ.

The result

A major challenge presented itself during the project: finding an appropriate permanent location for a fuel station. The fuel station would need certain utilities and would have to be easily accessible from both water and land.

The originally intended location, on Shell's grounds, turned out to be unsuitable. The procedures took too long. By then, Shell's staff was taking the public ferry to cross the river. The boat, which had cost over two million euros, was sidelined.

The aftermath

The boat was eventually put into service as a tour boat in 2011—but other problems arose. The boat is too expensive to operate, the price of fossil fuels is very low, and the boat's length of 72 feet exceeds the new limit set by the municipality of Amsterdam: Tour boats shouldn't be longer than 65.6 feet.

5. *The Empty Seat at the Table* (not all relevant parties are involved)

All relevant parties must agree with a change in order for it to succeed. If a party isn't involved in the preparation or implementation, chances are this party won't be convinced of the usefulness or importance of the change due to a lack of involvement. The sense of exclusion can also lead to a lack of cooperation. This also applies to customers who feel like their voices haven't been heard in the development of new products. The term "fair process" is used to indicate that people are more likely to accept a result—whether positive or negative—when they're well informed and their interests have been taken into account. This is why it's important to conduct a stakeholder analysis to determine who may be affected by a project and to subsequently involve these people in the right way, from the beginning of the project to its eventual implementation to avoid having empty seats at the table.

Hotline to home

Hotline to Home was a telecom project initiated by a cardiologist in a small peripheral hospital in the Netherlands, aimed at improving inpatients' wellbeing by increasing and maintaining important social contacts through a combination of new technology and communication volunteers.

Technological solutions ultimately stand or fall on acceptance by their eventual beneficiaries. That's why the enthusiasm of experts and visionaries does not guarantee the success of a new technological solution in the field of communication. First, the wishes and opportunities of the intended users must be thoroughly researched.

6. The Bear's Skin (concluding too quickly that success has been achieved)

Initial success can lead us to mistakenly believe that we've chosen the right path. Sustainable success, however, requires an approach to work in the longer term, on a larger scale, and/or in other circumstances as well. In fact, initial success may hinder us from finding the right longer-term approach, as it means we're not incentivized or forced to explore alternatives or potential longer-term obstacles. This can be seen very clearly in the start-up world, in which rapid initial growth doesn't guarantee a healthy business in the longer term. For many companies, the step from proof of concept to proof of business is a big step—often even too big a step. This is not surprising in light of the differences between these two phases in the life cycle of a young company. Almost everything is different, from the skills required in the team and the type of customers, to the type of financing and the governance structure. This requires more than a good idea or interesting technology; it requires the ability to adapt the organization to the phase it's currently in. Of course, this doesn't just apply to start-ups. In sports, for example, a strategy or technique that was initially successful often has to be unlearned with great difficulty later because it prevents further development. The Dutch equivalent of the saying "Don't count your chickens before they hatch" serves as a powerful metaphor for these kinds of situations: "Don't sell the skin before the bear has been shot."

Broken Windows, Broken Lives

The intention
In the nineties, people wanted to restore order in major American cities.

The approach
The then mayor of New York City, Rudy Giulliani, implemented a zero tolerance policy, inspired by the work of two

criminologists, George Kelling and James Q. Wilson (1982), who'd introduced the so-called broken windows theory. This meant that the police started targeting small-time offenders as well as major criminals, based on the idea that not addressing petty crime (breaking a window of a building) will cause the entire neighborhood to deteriorate (the whole building will be run down). Other cities were impressed and adopted the same approach.

The result
The approach was initially successful: Crime rates declined. This method would serve as a model of an effective approach to crime and deterioration for several decades. It transpired, however, that the police were rather overzealous in enforcing the policy, resulting in overcrowded prisons and social unrest,with protesters chanting "Broken Windows, Broken Lives". There was a kind of witch-hunt against small-time offenders, and even people who hadn't done anything wrong— Black Americans in particular—were sometimes harassed by the police.

The lessons learned
Don't be blinded by initial success; check whether your approach is sustainable in the longer term or at a larger scale. After a while, also check whether your approach needs to be modified. Even George Kelling eventually had to admit that their concept wasn't sustainable without modifications.

7. *The Light Bulb* (experimenting)

Progress usually doesn't follow a linear path. This is why we have to try, experiment, and learn in order to find the best approach or the right road to success.

We don't always have all necessary information either. Sometimes the situation is complex, as a result of which not all relevant issues and interconnections can be known and can only be found through trial and error. Our failed attempts at the very least tell us how something *shouldn't* be done or help us discover things that could inform the design and/or execution of our next attempt. This does, however, require the willingness and ability to fail and to be open to learning experiences. Einstein already said, "If we knew what we were doing, we wouldn't call it research." Another great mind, Thomas Edison, also recognized the importance of experimentation, learning, and trial and error.

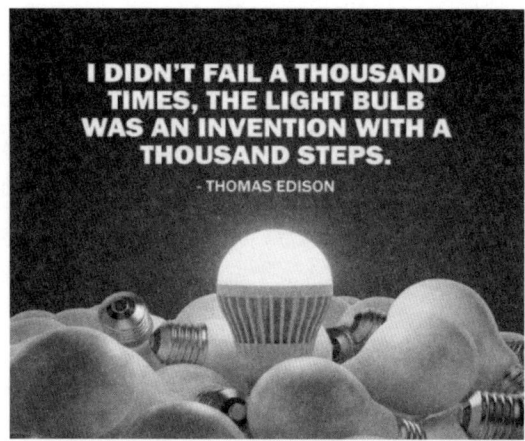

I DIDN'T FAIL A THOUSAND TIMES, THE LIGHT BULB WAS AN INVENTION WITH A THOUSAND STEPS.
- THOMAS EDISON

Playing around with pencils and sticky tape
www.briljantemislukkingen.nl/en/2012/02/06/nobelprize- by-playing-with-pencil-and-scotch-tape/

Physicists Geim and Novoselov enjoyed organizing their so-called Friday night experiments: fun experiments without preconceived scenarios to which you should devote "at least 10 percent of your time," they said in an interview. In one such experiment in 2004, they used a piece of Scotch tape to peel an extremely thin flake of graphite off the tip of a pencil and ended up with graphene, a honeycomb structure of carbon atoms that continues to intrigue the world of physics to this day. It also won Geim and Novoselov the Nobel Prize in Physics 2010.

8. *The General Without an Army* (the right idea, but not the resources)

Achieving the planned success requires the necessary resources to be available. These may include money, the right instruments, knowledge, time, employees, partners, customers or clients, and infrastructure. The party or parties providing these resources must sufficiently commit to the party or parties performing the activities. Parties may include management, investors, loyal customers, colleagues, and others who can contribute something relevant to the success of the project. Of course, no single resource is infinitely available, and every entrepreneur is faced with the task and challenge of making optimum use of available resources. Sometimes it turns out that people have been undertaking an impossible mission because the most indispensable support and resources are unavailable. It's nice to play a significant role, but even the most capable person can't achieve any success without the necessary resources.

Xerox PARC: great ideas, but no execution power

Copy machine manufacturer Xerox wanted to enter the field of computers, especially printers. They came up with the computer mouse, the Ethernet (and therefore the Internet), a graphical user interface, and a WYSIWYG editor—in other words, everything a modern computer needs. But the company didn't have a marketing plan or sales method in place, which meant a lack of support and resources. After a tour of Xerox PARC, Steve Jobs felt greatly inspired by Xerox's ideas, and the rest is history.

9. *The Junk* (the art of stopping)

It's very human to want to finish what we started. After all, we set goals for a reason. Statements such as "quitting is not in my vocabulary," "you can do this" and "a deal is a deal" show the human dimension of the "unable or unwilling to stop" syndrome. But sometimes it's because of business considerations that a project isn't discontinued before its goal has been reached or before it can really no longer be continued. It's not always easy to declare a project unsuccessful, so you try as long as possible to make something of it. Or you try to rescue your revenue. A well-known fallacious justification for continuing activities and related investments is the so-called sunk cost fallacy. People consider the investments they've already made and conclude that it would be a shame to have made all those investments for nothing. But you should look ahead rather than back: how many investments still have to be made and what will you get in return? Also, you can earn back some of the losses by evaluating and applying the lessons learned in the future. Instead of "failure costs," you'll get "failure returns."

Turn failed IT projects into Brilliant Failures

Contribution by Paul Iske, Frank Harmsen, Hans Mulder, Maurice Nijssen & Frits Bussemaker

The Dutch Personal Records Database (BRP) contains the personal data of people who live in the Netherlands and Dutch people who live abroad. The debacle of modernizing this database, the so-called BRP project, is one in a long line of failed IT projects initiated by the Dutch government. It seems like a lot of money is being spent inefficiently, which is a severe matter. What's even worse is that the government seems unable to learn from its mistakes. This is why we are calling for failed IT projects to be turned into Brilliant Failures.

The findings presented by the Elias Committee, a temporary parliamentary committee formed a few years ago to investigate failed IT government projects on behalf of the Dutch House of Representatives, caused a wave of indignation in both politics and Dutch society in general: "A waste of taxpayers' money! This has to change!" The Committee's recommendations were aimed at preventing failure. For example, the Bureau of IT Testing (BIT) was established to examine each larger and high-risk government project with an IT component and make recommendations for improving a project's chances of success. It was partly because of the advice of the BIT that the BRP project was eventually discontinued.

Neither the Elias Committee nor the BIT could prevent the BRP project from stagnating and continuing for too long, resulting in a loss of ninety million euros. Well-known pitfalls were at play: too much complexity, a need that changed over time, and an approach that insufficiently took this changing need into account, as a result of which no one had a clear overview anymore and the project became uncontrollable.

10. The Canyon (ingrained patterns)

We often encounter the same situations over and over in our lives. To efficiently deal with these situations, we develop routines, habits and best practices. Both individually and organizationally we acquire abilities, which—consciously or unconsciously—become embedded in our brains or in written and unwritten protocols in the organization or in society. On the one hand, this is useful and necessary. Imagine feeling like you're experiencing something for the first time every time you do it! That way, we wouldn't be able to enjoy the benefits of experience and development. It also gives us part of our identity and authority: "This is how we do it and this is how we learned to do it." But on the other hand, there's a certain risk involved in blindly relying on our experiences. What if there are other, better ways to go about things? Or what if the environment or issue changes? What if we become too limited in our thinking, failing to see new opportunities and new threats—or what if we do see them, but are no longer capable of generating new solutions? Compare it to a river that has been running through an area of land for millions of years. Over this time, it may have carved a beautiful canyon and created an awesome landscape, such as the Grand Canyon. But to the river, the world has become narrowed down. Everything that happens outside the canyon is completely hidden from the view of the river and its inhabitants.

Conference on alternative treatments for gastrointestinal problems
Contribution by Marc Benninga ("The Poop Doctor")

The intention
Pediatricians are increasingly asked by parents whether complementary medicine could be a suitable alternative treatment for their child with medical problems. Recent research has shown that between 40 and 60 percent of children with gastrointestinal problems already make use of or have

previously made use of complementary medicine (homeopathy, bioresonance, iridology, acupuncture and osteopathy). As my knowledge in this area is very limited, I was unable to provide parents with much useful information. This was the reason for me to organize a symposium at which complementary medical practitioners and clinical epidemiologists would be asked to present their experiences, scientific arguments, and views with regard to complementary medicine.

The approach
Homeopaths, acupuncturists, osteopaths and bioresonance practitioners were asked which gastroenterological indications their treatments were used for; the pathophysiological basis of the treatments; what exactly the treatments involved; the duration of the treatments; the potential side effects or risks; the costs; and whether patients were insured for the treatments. Clinical epidemiologists were asked to discuss the scientific basis of the indications and treatments.

The symposium would be part of an annual training day for pediatric residents, pediatricians, child psychologists, pediatric nurses, family physicians and pediatric physiotherapists. Information about this day was communicated by the Amsterdam-based European Postgraduate Gastro-surgical School (EPGS).

The result
After the invitation, the provisional program was sent out and the then chair of the Executive Board of the Academic Medical Center (AMC) in Amsterdam called me to make an appointment. A vehement opponent of complementary medicine had tipped her off about a symposium on complementary medicine that was to take place at the AMC. In our conversation, she made it plain that the AMC did not wish to be associated with complementary medicine and that the

symposium had to be canceled. At the same time, it became clear that none of the professors of epidemiology I wanted to invite to share their views were eager to engage with this touchy subject. Perhaps they were of the same opinion as the then chair of the Executive Board.

The lessons learned
Conventional medicine in the Netherlands wasn't—and per-haps still isn't—prepared to discuss this important subject in an informative, scientific, and objective way.

And there's more...
At present, dietary and medicinal treatments of chronic abdominal pain in children have rarely been studied. More-over, studies show limited effectiveness. In the last ten years, we've conducted large randomized clinical trials in which children with chronic abdominal pain received hypnotherapy. Against all my expectations, this treatment was very suc-cessful in both the short term and the long term. One-year follow-up results showed that 85 percent of the children with abdominal pain who had received hypnotherapy were cured, compared to only 25 percent of the children who had been treated by a pediatric gastroenterologist. The results of these studies, which were conducted according to the principles of evidence-based medicine and published in leading interna-tional journals, are viewed with suspicion by practitioners of conventional medicine. It's true that we don't yet know why exactly hypnotherapy is such an effective treatment for this specific group of patients. However, it's now up to conventio-nal medicine to provide a scientific answer to this question. Our research group is currently working on this.

11. *The Right Hemisphere* (not all decisions are made on rational grounds)

The behavior of a complex system is often difficult to predict. It becomes even more difficult to predict when the individual behavior of parties in the system cannot be (directly) explained based on known facts. Some people are unpredictable and/or inconsistent in their reactions and decisions, which introduces an additional degree of uncertainty. In some cultures, it's quite normal for people to change their minds without any external change. It may also be difficult for people to gather all the facts or process them objectively, resulting in selective or out-of-context use of facts. And sometimes people mistakenly believe they completely understand the situation. Interestingly, though perhaps not surprisingly, this phenomenon also occurs when major decisions have to be made. Sometimes the issue is so large and complex that not all uncertainties can be removed due to a lack of time (or willingness), in which case people prefer to rely on intuition and experience. Others—who have no insight into the other party's internal considerations or don't know on which facts the other party is basing their decisions—may become confused and, in turn, base their decisions on assumptions about the other party's thinking and decision-making processes. In their book *Sway: The Irresistible Pull of Irrational Behavior* (2008), brothers Ori and Rom Brafman describe underlying patterns that lead to irrational behavior.

Warren Buffett's two-hundred-billion-dollar mistake

The intention
In the sixties, famous investor and billionaire Warren Buffett wanted to make money through a series of investments in textile company Berkshire Hathaway. The company had been in decline for years and was closing mills with some regularity. It used the proceeds to purchase its own stock, driving up the value.

The approach
Just before another textile mill was closed, Buffett's investment entity,which would now be called a hedge fund, invested significantly in Berkshire Hathaway. In 1964 Buffett spoke with Seabury Stanton, the then CEO of the company, and agreed to tender his stock to the company for 11.50 dollars after the closure of a number of mills.

The result
A few weeks later, Buffett was mailed a tender offer by Berkshire Hathaway. The company offered to buy his stock for $11^3/_8$ dollars, $^1/_8$ of a dollar less than the agreed-upon price of 11.50 dollars. Angered, Buffett bought more stock, took control of the company, and fired Stanton. He was consequently stuck with a relatively unprofitable textile business for years. Buffett claims this move ultimately cost him two hundred billion dollars, as he couldn't invest the money in a more profitable business or investment company.

The lessons learned
Allowing your decisions to be overly influenced by emotions such as revenge, although this goes against rational considerations, is asking for trouble. In situations like these, it would be wise to count to ten before making a decision.

12. *The Banana Peel* (accidents happen)
Complex situations involve many parties influencing each other. It's not always easy to determine which effects elsewhere in the system are the result of a change at a local level. Remember the myth of the butterfly that flapped its wings and caused a storm on another continent? Although this certainly doesn't happen every day, it's true that life is ultimately

largely determined by the sum of the effects of relatively minor events. We tend to focus on matters of great or immediate concern, paying less attention to events that may also trigger system-level phenomena. An example of such an approach is scenario planning. Although this method is about considering potential developments with a major impact, scenario projects also involve identifying early warning systems. In complex situations, the trick is to notice and evaluate minor, sometimes seemingly irrelevant facts. It's also useful to assess the vulnerability of the activity to small deviations from the ideal or expected situation. You only have to watch the news to see how often people—literally or figuratively—slip on relatively minor or trivial things.

Buckler beer on the Dutch market
In the summer of 1988, Dutch brewing company Heineken launched a low-alcohol beer (0.5 percent). The company opted for low-alcohol beer because it feared consumers would not be interested in alcohol-free beer. A strong brand name was chosen: Buckler. Buckler beer was initially successful, capturing a large share of the low-alcohol beer market both nationally and internationally. Five years after its launch, however, Buckler was taken off the Dutch market. Youp van 't Hek, now one of the most famous comedians in the Netherlands, had ruthlessly mocked Buckler drinkers during a widely watched New Year's Eve cabaret performance in 1989: "You know who I really can't stand? People who drink Buckler beer. Buckler, you know—orthodox Protestant beer. Forty-something jackasses standing next to you at the bar with their car keys in their hands. Get lost, man, I'm trying to get wasted here! Get out of here, moron, why don't you go drink that in a church, you idiot? You might as well not drink at all, you idiot, you BUCKLER drinker." It had a disastrous impact on the brand's national image.

13. *The Farmer's Daughter* (the power of serendipity)

A divergent outcome often doesn't meet expectations and is considered to be a failure at first. But on closer inspection, the result may turn out to be valuable in a different way. There are various famous examples of this Brilliant Failure archetype, such as 3M's Post-it Note: A weak adhesive—initially considered a failure—turned out to be the perfect ingredient for sticking things together and easily pulling them apart again. Another previously mentioned example is the erectile dysfunction drug Viagra, originally intended as a treatment for heart failure and angina pectoris. Talk about finding something while looking for something else...

Post-it®

3M scientist Spence Silver developed an adhesive consisting of tiny spheres of glue in the hope of creating a strong, useful adhesive. Because of the small area of contact between the microspheres and a flat surface, the resulting layer is adhesive yet easy to peel off again. Silver was disappointed with the result, though; this new adhesive was even weaker than 3M's development efforts so far. 3M shelved the technology.

Four years later, one of Silver's colleagues at 3M, Art Fry, was frustrated by the bookmarks that kept falling out of his hymn book. He had a eureka moment and came up with the idea of using Silver's self-adhesive agent to make a reliable bookmark. The idea of the Post-it® note was born.

In 1981, one year after the introduction of Post-it® notes, the product was named 3M's Outstanding New Product. In addition to the classic sticky notes, various other Post-it® products have been released.

14. *The Einstein Point* (dealing with complexity)

When undertaking activities in our complex world, we are constantly faced with the challenge of making sure we have enough information for our view of the situation to be representative of reality. At the same time, our approach shouldn't become so complicated that we are no longer able to link cause and effect and end up in a "black box" situation, having essentially lost control.

We should neither oversimplify nor overcomplicate situations. When we oversimplify a situation, we tend to generate solutions that won't work in practice; when we overcomplicate a situation, we run the risk of becoming paralyzed. As Einstein already said, "Everything should be made as simple as possible, but not simpler." The trick, then, is to determine the point at which our view of the situation is as simple as possible, but still representative of reality. In other words, we have to keep an eye on the Einstein Point.

Brexit

A good example of a situation in which the Einstein Point seems to have been lost from sight is Brexit, the United Kingdom's decision to leave the European Union based on the outcome of a referendum in June 2016. This decision was made with only a small majority of votes, by the way, and with young people in particular voting to remain in the EU. It soon became clear that not everyone fully understood the consequences of this decision at the time of voting.

On the one hand, voters were influenced by those who wanted the United Kingdom to remain in the European Union. They tried to tell the whole story, which was too complicated, abstract or macro-level for many people. These people, for example, who feel like they experience the disadvantages of globalization but not the advantages. For this reason, they preferred to listen to more populist views, which oversimplified the situation and described solutions that would not work in practice. The discussion between these parties with positions on either side of the Einstein Point led to a seemingly impossible decision being made anyway, with all the ensuing consequences that will reach far into the future.

15. *The Acapulco Cliff Diver* (timing)

When is the right time to do something? Introducing new products or services in particular is not just a matter of having a good idea, but also of waiting for the right moment. It often happens that someone feels like they have a great idea, but then it turns out a similar development has already taken place and a similar proposition has just reached the market; or the market has already changed again. This is why it's dangerous to spend too much time contemplating an innovation or striving for perfection. Sometimes good is good enough. But the opposite often happens as well: Someone is the first to come up with a fantastic innovation, but then it turns out the market isn't ready for it yet. Sometimes people have to get used to a new approach, sometimes preconditions haven't been met, and sometimes a new product has too many teething problems. After all, too early isn't on time, either... This is reminiscent of the famous cliff divers in Acapulco, Mexico, who dive into the sea from great heights, often in front of a huge audience. They have to wait for the right moment, when an incoming wave sufficiently increases the water level. You can imagine what would happen if their timing was off. For the divers, this sense of timing is just as important as their diving technique itself.

Rotterdam SkillCity
Contribution by Henk Oosterling

The intention
Rotterdam SkillCity is a project aimed at putting ambitious and sustainable craftsmanship based on 21st century skills on the map in the city of Rotterdam throughout the entire educational trajectory.

The approach
Rotterdam SkillCity propagates a threefold interpretation of ecology ("Eco3 education"): systematically developing physically, mentally, and socially sustainable thinking and acting in students. Such "eco-wisdom" could become the core of the regular primary education curriculum. This approach has been successfully developed at four elementary schools in socioeconomically weaker neighborhoods in Rotterdam between 2008 and now. From the first year of school onward, children take classes in cooking and gardening and weekly classes in judo, technology and philosophy. Parents along with vocational and university trainees are directly involved with these classes. This elementary school program was scaled up to secondary education after two years, and then to vocational education two years after that.

The result
This ecosocial approach is rooted in two educational projects that, in retrospect, can be considered Brilliant Failures. The first experiment took place between 1975 and 1977; the second experiment took place between 1981 and 1983. In 1975 I set up a similar, though smaller-scale, educational project together with teachers, staff and parents at an elementary school in the same neighborhood where Rotterdam SkillCity would be launched in 2008. This neighborhood had become

increasingly multicultural in the preceding decade, as a result of which its school population and educational demands had changed. A then-innovative approach in which the school developed its own learning materials also caused the hierarchical relationships between management, teachers, support staff and parents to disappear. Behavioral and learning problems were adequately dealt with. But the project was called off two years later by the Rotterdam city council, despite its having the approval of the Dutch Inspectorate of Education, its active parent participation, and the successes achieved. The project was considered too radical and rebellious. All teachers were fired. Apparently, the time wasn't right yet.

Five years later, I initiated a primary education "eco-project" about alternative, sustainable energy sources, decentralized environmental management and a healthy lifestyle. It was a time of squatter riots, high unemployment, and a wide public debate about nuclear energy in the Netherlands. We again managed to involve the municipality and a core team of teachers who tested the classes. In 1983, we delivered a comprehensive package of classes and a teaching manual. But although the materials were used at petting zoos for more than ten years, they were never adopted into the regular primary education curriculum. In the early nineties, petting zoos stopped using them as well.

Learning from a Brilliant Failure
Looking back on those "failures" in 1975 and 1983, I don't think I could've done anything differently at the time. In retrospect—knowing what I didn't know at the time—everything could've been done differently and better, of course. But hindsight is always twenty-twenty. Never underestimate the powers that be and never overestimate yourself, either. Always work in a collective and create an increasing amount

of support among a diversity of stakeholders. With Rotterdam SkillCity, I managed to find the right timing from the point of view of "the powers that be." Adapting to existing policy is the first step in any innovation. But this adaptation must always be aimed at a more integral connection and, eventually, at a transition in which the other party can recognize itself.

The opportunity to implement something that couldn't be done a few decades ago presented itself between 2004 and 2006: Never waste a good crisis! This time, however, we were much better prepared. The Eco3 educational system was grafted onto the city's policy jargon. We talked with directors and policy makers, formed coalitions with neighborhood partners, and worked with local groups of youths. Continuous strategic, tactical, and operational adjustment creates an increasing amount of support for this educational innovation, which was established in 2008 and is still being developed.

16. *The Winner Takes it All* (room for only one solution)

Although the world in general and innovation in particular benefit from diversity and competition, sometimes there's only room for one dominant party. Think of standards, for example. People sometimes think that having to comply with standards is the opposite of creativity and innovation, but this isn't true. Manufacturers know that if their product is compliant—that is, widely applicable—and there is no standard, products may have much less reach. Isn't it very convenient to have such a thing as a GSM standard, which allows cell phones of any brand to communicate with each other? Or that a 110-volt or 230-volt appliance works virtually everywhere. It is just unfortunate that there's no global voltage standard with a universal power plug, or is it? With some kinds of entrepreneurial activities, it's clear in advance or very early in the process that there will be room for only one winning party, which will set the standard or be able to develop the most-used platform. This party isn't necessarily the best party, by the way, but the party with the winning combination of quality, strategy, and influence at that particular moment in time. A classic example is the videotape format war (VHS, V2000, Betamax), in which commercial quality ultimately won out over technical quality. Sometimes people deliberately create a situation in which it's determined in advance that only one party's efforts will be rewarded. In software development, for example, people sometimes engage in concurrent development: multiple teams simultaneously trying to program the same functionality. This guarantees progress, but it also means that the work of unselected teams won't be used yet.

The famous Swedish pop group ABBA eloquently expressed this in their song "The Winner Takes it All," in which the following combination of phrases occurs: "The winner takes it all, the loser standing small." Although this is often the case, we should be glad that people aren't discouraged by it and continue to compete even in red oceans (competitive environments) to keep striving for improvement and challenging the position of the dominant parties.

Video 2000 versus VHS

Video 2000 was a video standard developed by Philips and Grundig to compete with VHS and Betamax. It surpassed both formats in terms of quality and duration. The Video 2000 system was technologically superior to both Betamax and VHS, but it reached the market too late; the VHS standard had already established itself as the dominant home video system, and Philips and Grundig were unable to take over this position.

The Elephant	The Black Swan	The Wrong Wallet	The Bridge of Choluteca
The whole is greater than the sum of its parts	Unforeseen developments are part of the game	One person's advantage is another person's disadvantage	Problems don't stay in one place

The Empty Seat at the Table	The Bear's Skin	The Light Bulb	The General Without an Army
Not all relevant parties are involved	Concluding too quickly that success has been achieved	"If we knew what we were doing, we wouldn't call it research"	The right idea, but not the resources

The Junk	The Canyon	The Right Hemisphere	The Banana Peel
The art of stopping	Ingrained patterns	Not all decisions are made on rational grounds	Accidents happen

The Farmer's Daughter	The Einstein Point	The Acapulco Cliff Diver	The Winner Takes it All
The art of accidentally discovering something important	Dealing with complexity	Timing	Room for only one solution

Figure 13 contains an overview of the sixteen archetypes.

Failing and Learning at Various Levels

The archetypes can help us determine exactly where and why matters took an unexpected turn. To be even better able to recognize and benefit from the value of Brilliant Failures, it's important to distinguish between four different levels of learning:

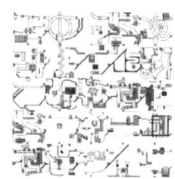

1. *System failure* (failure due to the properties of the system): In this case, things don't go as expected or desired because of the rules that govern the behavior of the system. These may, for example, result in perverse incentives that cause behavior at a local level that is undesirable for the system as a whole. Or they may result in long-term effects or side effects that prevent the original goals from being achieved. Finally, a system may become so complex that people are no longer able to see and/or understand the relationship between cause and effect.

2. *Organizational failure* (failure at the organizational level): Subsets of the system may be organized in such a way that they make it impossible for the goals that have been set to be achieved. These organizations may have rules and/or cultures that are incompatible with the goals set. In organizations, the use of a management model that is unsuitable for the business activity in question could easily result in failure. For example, there may be a lack of cooperation between the various parts of the organization, or the organization may not possess the knowledge necessary for a project to succeed due to an inadequate HR policy. Other components of the system or other parties have little or no influence on this.

3. *Team failure* (failure due to team-level deficiencies): Many business activities are carried out in teams. For optimum performance, it's important that members of a team complement each other. They must have complementary skills and together be able to achieve the goals that have been set, based on trust and common ambitions and by utilizing the diversity of the team. Sometimes, however, not all relevant knowledge is present in the team or not all knowledge is being used to the fullest extent. The latter may be a result of various reasons: There may be a lack of time, a lack of trust, no common ambitions, or the team may be trying to achieve consensus too quickly, rendering it blind to other possibilities. The functioning of a team may also be influenced by its environment, that is, the organization or system.

4. *Individual failure* (failure due to individual deficiencies): No one is perfect and no one can have a complete overview of all the facts and developments. We all have our preferences and our ingrained ways of working and thinking, and we're not always rational when it comes to making decisions. The "Dirty Dozen" factors identified by the aviation industry, as discussed in Chapter 2, are just twelve of the reasons why people may fail.

A Brilliant Failure may be the result of failure at one of the four levels, but it may also be the result of failure at two or three levels simultaneously. Combining these levels with the sixteen archetypes, we end up with a 16 x 4 matrix in which Brilliant Failures can be placed at various points.

On January 4, 2018, Hawaii was thrown into a panic: the nuclear warning system went off, and it clearly wasn't a scheduled test time. Commotion ensued, especially since tensions over the North Korean nuclear missile program had increased significantly. It quickly became clear that it was a misunderstanding; an employee had pushed the wrong button while resetting the system after maintenance. Fortunately, the mistake was quickly discovered before the U.S. reacted to this non-existent act of aggression, with potentially catastrophic consequences. The employee in question was fired, but is that really fair? Isn't it much more troubling that he was working with a system in which one mistake could have led to a disaster, and terrified a lot of people? This was definitely a case of system failure as well. It might actually have been better to keep the employee on: It seems very unlikely that he'll make the same mistake again.

Applying Chapter 5

1. Come up with examples of failures for as many archetypes as possible. You get three points for each of your own failures and one point for examples of other people's failures. Ask a few people around you to do the same.

2. Think of one or more failures in your own life and determine which archetype or archetypes they fit.

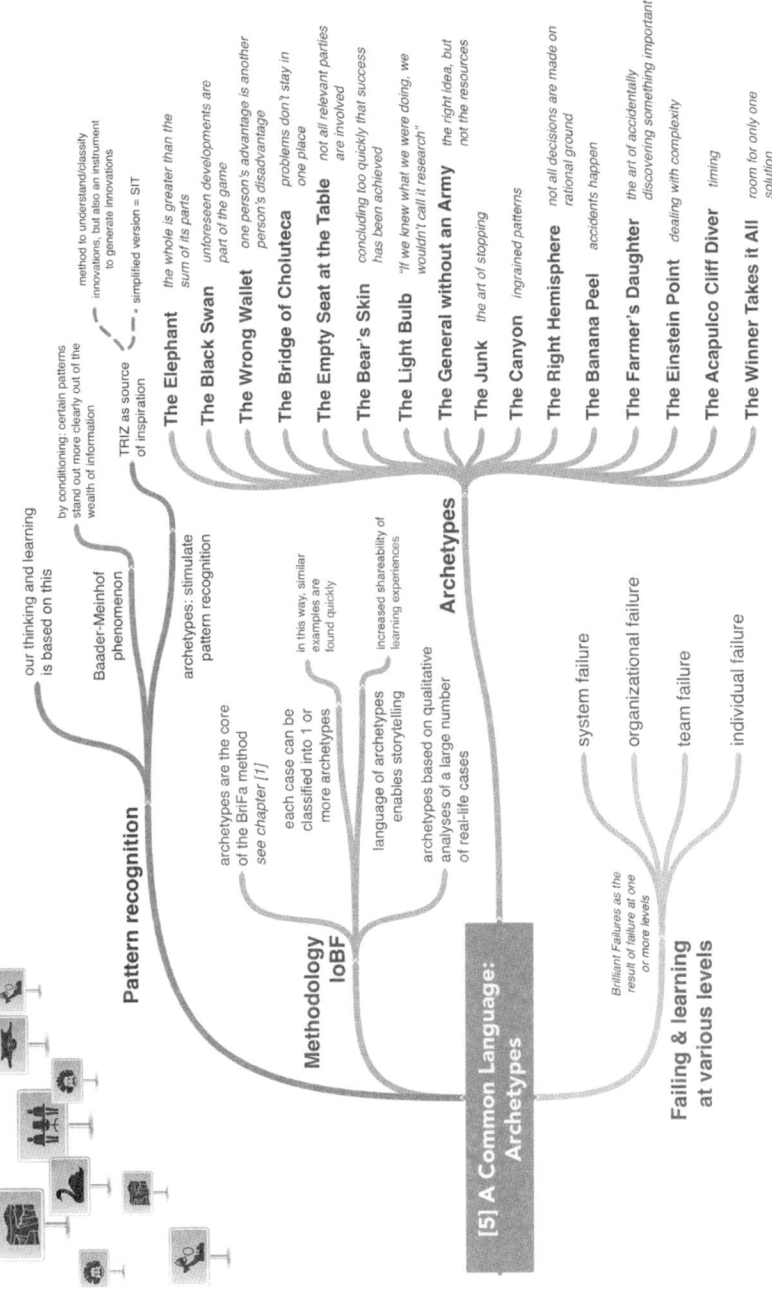

[5] A Common Language: Archetypes

Pattern recognition

- our thinking and learning is based on this
- Baader-Meinhof phenomenon
  - by conditioning: certain patterns stand out more clearly out of the wealth of information
- archetypes: stimulate pattern recognition

Methodology IoBF

- archetypes are the core of the BriFa method *see chapter [1]*
- TRIZ as source of inspiration
  - method to understand/classify innovations, but also an instrument to generate innovations
  - simplified version = SIT
- each case can be classified into 1 or more archetypes
  - in this way, similar examples are found quickly
- language of archetypes enables storytelling
  - increased shareability of learning experiences
- archetypes based on qualitative analyses of a large number of real-life cases

Archetypes

- **The Elephant** *the whole is greater than the sum of its parts*
- **The Black Swan** *unforeseen developments are part of the game*
- **The Wrong Wallet** *one person's advantage is another person's disadvantage*
- **The Bridge of Choluteca** *problems don't stay in one place*
- **The Empty Seat at the Table** *not all relevant parties are involved*
- **The Bear's Skin** *concluding too quickly that success has been achieved*
- **The Light Bulb** *"If we knew what we were doing, we wouldn't call it research"*
- **The General without an Army** *the right idea, but not the resources*
- **The Junk** *the art of stopping*
- **The Canyon** *ingrained patterns*
- **The Right Hemisphere** *not all decisions are made on rational ground*
- **The Banana Peel** *accidents happen*
- **The Farmer's Daughter** *the art of accidentally discovering something important*
- **The Einstein Point** *dealing with complexity*
- **The Acapulco Cliff Diver** *timing*
- **The Winner Takes it All** *room for only one solution*

Failing & learning at various levels

Brilliant Failures as the result of failure at one or more levels

- system failure
- organizational failure
- team failure
- individual failure

6. ON KNOWLEDGE AND LEARNING

Knowledge Makes the World Go Round

Knowledge plays an important role in virtually everything we do. Many people engage in a rather knowledge-intensive process once or several times a year without consciously realizing it: going on vacation. It's interesting to consider this relaxing activity from a knowledge perspective. Let's list all the things you have to do, decide and know in order to have a reasonable chance of a successful trip with or without your family.

Type of action	Description	Knowledge necessary	Sources of knowledge
Deciding	What are we going to do?	1. Preferences 2. Limitations 3. Experiences	1. Family members 2. Family members 3. Family, friends, Internet
Deciding	Where and when are we going?	1. Preferences 2. Possible dates 3. Climate information 4. Budget 5. Activities on offer 6. Availability	1. Family members 2. Calendars, Internet 3. Internet, travel guides 4. Bank statements 5. Travel guides, Internet 6. Travel agency, Internet
Doing	Planning and booking	1. Where to book 2. Prices 3. Availability	1. Internet, travel agency 2. Internet, travel agency 3. Internet, travel agency
Doing	Preparing	1. What to bring 2. Items to buy 3. How much can we bring? 4. Who can pet-sit? 5. Transport (cab)	1. Lists, family members 2. Pantry, Internet, store 3. Transporter's terms and conditions, experience 4. Family, neighbors, Internet 5. Internet, list of contacts, friends/acquaintances
Doing	Going on vacation	1. Travel information 2. Accommodation 3. Activities 4. Food: where, what, prices 5. Purchases: what, shopping hours, prices 6. Monitoring home situation	1. Booking information, Internet, tourist information center 2. Booking information, travel planner 3. Booking information, experience, Internet, tourist information 4. Experience, Internet, recommendations 5. Experience, local information, currency information 6. People at home, social media, news, Internet, webcams
Doing	Going home	1. Financial overview 2. Home situation 3. Action points	1. Bank/credit card statements 2. Contact with people at home 3. Email, to do list, experience

Table 1. Vacation: A knowledge-intensive process

Good intentions and preparations notwithstanding, your vacation may turn out differently than planned or desired. This may be for a variety of reasons, such as disappointing weather, poor organization at your place of destination, or conflicts within your family. Maybe your past experiences are no longer relevant in the present; maybe the city is busier than you expected; maybe your cat gets sick, your flight gets delayed, or your family gets food poisoning; maybe you return home to a huge backlog of work, ended up spending too much money after all, and so on and so forth. Some of these things may be preventable and others may be caused primarily by external and uncertain factors. Some things may have been knowable in advance, whereas others were not.

These are the makings of a Brilliant Failure: Your intentions are good, you're prepared, you do your best, and yet things don't always go as intended.

The more knowledge used in the preparation stage, the greater the chance that the unexpected result is something interesting rather than something predictable that could easily have been prevented. Moreover, you've generated new knowledge by acting. You've gained experiences, which are often valuable in their own right, but can become even more valuable if you also manage to use them in a subsequent activity and share them with others who also benefit from them.

In order to describe more clearly the relationship between Brilliant Failures, knowledge and learning, it's useful to clarify the term "knowledge." For our purposes, knowledge can be seen as the "fuel" for performing tasks to which decision making, creating opportunities, and problem solving are central. Knowledge comes in three different categories: insights–past experiences, understanding through reflection; information–data collected and presented in such a way that it can be given meaning, reducing ignorance, uncertainty or indeterminacy; and inspiration–which tells us where we want or need to go. Roughly speaking, we use knowledge to connect the past, the present, and the future. These three elements can be combined into a simple formula:

$K = I \times I \times I$ (Knowledge is Insights x Information x Inspiration).

Information, also known as explicit knowledge, can be divorced from its original context and shared through various channels, such as the Internet, books, databases and reports. The comparison, however, shows that an important part of knowledge lies within us. Our experiences are an important source of the insights and inspiration to do something or make a decision. Sometimes insights either can't or can hardly be put into words. This kind of knowledge that can't or almost can't be made explicit is known as tacit or implicit knowledge.

Knowledge as fuel

The analogy of knowledge as fuel for making decisions and performing tasks can be further developed by considering the fuel value chain. Petroleum has to be found, produced, transported, refined, distributed, pumped, and then burned to set a vehicle in motion. All of these steps are part of the "knowledge process" as well. The refining step, for example, is necessary for converting crude oil into a usable form, as you can't just pour crude oil into your car. Some oil fields become depleted, meaning new sources have to be found; this has to be anticipated and invested in well in advance. Another element of the metaphor involves the application of knowledge: The user must be willing to look for and invest in the fuel. For the time being, fuel doesn't hop into our cars by itself... It's often said that the greatest challenge of knowledge management is motivating people to share their knowledge. This, however, is only half the story; people also need to be motivated to seek knowledge.

The Knowledge Value Chain

By combining and using knowledge from various sources, we become increasingly capable. Or, as Isaac Newton said, "If I have seen further than others, it is because I was standing on the shoulders of giants."

In his 1997 book on knowledge management, Mathieu Weggeman provides a knowledge value chain describing the main steps that ensure the right knowledge is available and actually being used.

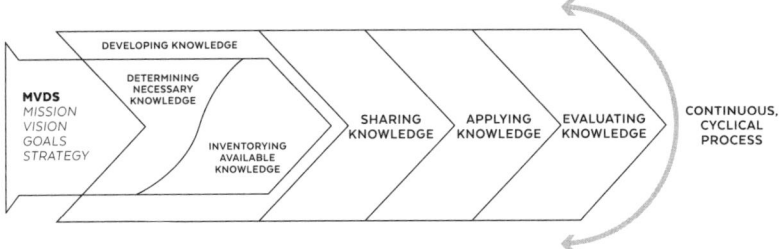

Figure 14. The knowledge value chain

The left part of the chain is primarily strategic in character: What do we want to achieve and what knowledge do we need in order to achieve it? Is this knowledge available and, if not, how will we acquire it through development, purchasing, cooperation, etc.? As we move toward the right side of the chain we enter the operational part, which considers how the knowledge can be made shareable and applicable. Every now and then we have to check whether the available knowledge is still relevant and of sufficient quality to achieve the goals that have been set. According to Weggeman, this is partially to do with the half-life of knowledge: the time after which half of the knowledge in an environment is no longer relevant. This brings us back to the strategic part, showing that the chain is actually a cycle.

In the knowledge economy, knowledge is the most important factor for future and sustainable success. Dealing with knowledge in a wrong or careless way results in the loss of much knowledge and therefore money. This may be due to employees leaving, poor transfer, disagreement, lack of coordination, or simply due to knowledge being buried so deep inside systems that it can no longer be accessed. Many organizations believe that knowledge should primarily be collected and made accessible through IT systems. In practice, though, this often results in a "databasement" where everything is stored and becomes hopelessly outdated over time. People will no longer know what's stored in the databasement and make less and less use of it, which doesn't make maintaining it any more appealing. This leads to a vicious circle.

The knowledge value chain shows that it's not just about the availability of the knowledge, but also about the ability to use said knowledge. It's about realizing the potential of the knowledge. It's very important that the necessary knowledge can be shared and used in an efficient and effective way, especially in situations involving people from different backgrounds and/or different companies or even different industries. This is only possible if the knowledge is not just accessible, but also consistently and unambiguously formulated. It should also be possible to evaluate the current relevance and accuracy of the knowledge.

"Can you estimate the percentage of your knowledge (insights, information, ideas) you use in your daily activities?" was a question in an online survey with 930 Dutch respondents from a wide variety of backgrounds. A respondent's answer to this question is a form of self-assessment, of course, and generally not based on a full understanding of knowledge quantification. It does, however, indicate the extent to which they believe more use could be made of the available knowledge. The results are shown in Figure 15.

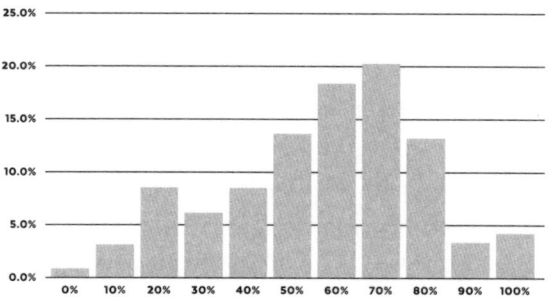

Figure 15. Can you estimate the percentage (x-axis) of your knowledge (insights, information, ideas) you use in your daily activities? (y-axis, N=930) [Iske (2004)]. For example, 20% of the 930 respondents estimate that they use 70% of their knowledge in their daily activities.

Our conclusion from this small study of the use of "personal intellectual capital" in organizations was that people's self-reported use of knowledge is just under 60 percent. There seems to be room for improvement here.

Knowledge Transfer

Only a small amount of all knowledge can be transferred through documents (codified knowledge). A cross-industry study by the Delphi Group showed that, on average, only 12 percent of all knowledge is codified knowledge. All other knowledge consists primarily of knowledge stored in "unstructured" knowledge environments, such as our brains and emails, notes, voicemails, etc.

The effectiveness of knowledge transfer would benefit greatly from an approach with the right balance between knowledge transfer through documents, codified knowledge, and an interactive way of sharing knowledge between the provider and the recipient of the knowledge. An interesting way of learning from each other could be provided by an expert panel. This is a system in which people can ask questions which are then directed to the most appropriate expert. There's also an increase in visual forms of knowledge transfer, such as the use of instructional videos.

Using the right approach and instruments can help knowledge gained in projects that Failed Brilliantly to "flow" more easily, allowing it to be used more often and in various places.

Chatbots are currently on the rise, leading people to the knowledge they're seeking via an automated question-and-answer conversation: a question-driven approach to acquiring knowledge. Asking questions has long been a powerful way to kickstart the process of sharing knowledge. In fact, it's the primary way through which children acquire knowledge. A good example of this is the website PatientsLikeMe (www.patientslike.com), where people can ask questions to experts, in this case often people who are or have been in the same situation.

Essentially, these kinds of applications help identify and catalog experts' experiences. This knowledge usually resides in the minds of the experts. It doesn't have to be described in detail, but gradually becomes more visible as the expert receives and answers more questions. There are various advantages to this approach:

a. Questions are asked on an as-needed basis: The context is clear and the feedback can be very direct.

b. The quality of the knowledge and the answers is immediately indicated by ratings (peer review).

c. Questions and answers remain in the system, which means they can be reused.

Practice has shown that this interactive way of acquiring and sharing knowledge has a high fun factor and is the killer application in many technological infrastructures. The approach also fits seamlessly within the BriFa method. The BriFa learning environment aims to extract knowledge from Brilliant Failures and make it easily shareable and applicable. This learning environment is both a system to which knowledge can be contributed and in which knowledge can be found and an information system which can tell you where knowledge can be found or where it's needed.

Much decision making, as it turns out, is based on tacit knowledge. This applies at the individual , team I and organizational level. Brilliant Failures also generate much tacit knowledge, which is not automatically available to others. In practice, this means that we need to find ways to share this knowledge with each other. Social interaction and reflection are important factors here.

According to Japanese scholars Ikujiro Nonaka and Hirotaka Takeuchi, the authors of *The Knowledge-Creating Company*, direct or indirect interaction between people is essential for spreading knowledge. Nonaka and Takeuchi have incorporated the various forms of knowledge transfer and knowledge accumulation into their so-called SECI model. SECI is an acronym for Socialization, Externalization, Combination, and Internalization, four processes that are essential for the continuous development and transfer of knowledge.

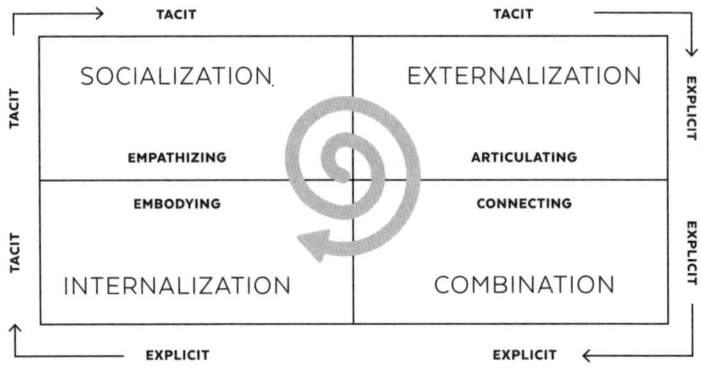

Figure 16. Nonaka and Takeuchi's SECI model of knowledge creation

Socialization

Socialization is sharing knowledge by gaining experience together or exchanging experiences. We share knowledge by working together, often without explicitly putting it into words. A well-known example of this form of knowledge sharing is the master andapprentice relationship, in which the apprentice learns from the master. People can also learn together in this way. Reflecting together on both positive and negative experiences allows us to draw conclusions about our own actions by comparing them to those of others.

Externalization

Externalization, or elicitation, is about making implicit knowledge as tangible as possible. This implicit knowledge may be either tacit, impossible to make explicit or not yet explicit. It's impossible to only share implicit knowledge with others through socialization. Making knowledge explicit makes it more concrete and more easily accessible to others. This may result in texts, sound or image exchanges.

Combination

Combination is about collecting and reorganizing explicit knowledge from various sources. It may also involve multiplying existing carriers of knowledge, such as making copies. Creating combinations may lead to new, transferable knowledge in the form of guidelines and standards, or training courses.

Internalization

Internalization is the process by which explicit knowledge is internalized. It then becomes part of someone's personal repertoire: The explicit knowledge is turned into a personal skill. This can be achieved by following a training course and applying what you learned in everyday practice, i.e. "learning by doing".

Successful knowledge transfer requires the right environment to be created. Nonaka and Takeuchi use the term "Ba," the Japanese word for space, to refer to this. Chapter 8 will elaborate on this concept.

Various Levels of Learning: Single-Loop and Double-Loop Learning
We'll now delve deeper into the phenomenon of learning, using the methodology developed by Argyris and Schön (1974, 1978). They distinguish between so-called single-loop and double-loop learning. Single-loop learning involves trying to determine what's going right or wrong with an action and actively trying to correct it. The resulting knowledge immediately takes you a step further. Double-loop learning involves learning at a higher level; in other words, it results in knowledge that can be used in the future and/or by other people. The "theory in use" is reviewed and adapted, allowing it to lead to the desired result later or elsewhere. Sometimes the original problem can no longer be solved, but the value is in the application of the knowledge to other situations.

What does "theory in use" mean? According to Argyris and Schön, people primarily act and evaluate based on their mental models, which are strongly influenced by their own experiences and preferences. These more unconscious driving forces are embedded in our actions and decisions and play a larger role than the theories we consciously espouse. Reflecting on our actions can enable us to identify and make explicit these "theories in use." Moreover, it allows us to better define and understand the differences between our espoused theories and our "theories in use."

A term that is sometimes used is deutero-learning. Deutero-learning involves a combination of single-loop and double-loop learning with the goal of learning in an even better and more conscious way. People learn from mistakes of both the present and the past and should be able to admit this.

The various aspects and levels of learning are also included in Kolb's (1984) so-called experiential learning cycle, which identifies four mechanisms of learning. These four mechanisms are:

1. Experience: Undergo or undertake a new action, with an open mind, single-loop learning.
2. Reflection: Look back on your experience in step 1. When you undertake a new action, some things go right and some things go wrong. Identify these things and consider them from various perspectives, double-loop learning, step 1.

3. Conceptualization: Are the experiences in steps 1 and 2 in line with the concept itself? Consider the relationship between these two steps, using your new experiences, double-loop learning, step 2.
4. Experimentation: Put the results of step 3 into practice. The results of this will again lead to new insights.

This whole process is a cycle. It keeps going, no matter where you start. Learning from a Brilliant Failure usually starts at step 4 and results in new knowledge that can be used at different times or in different places. Double-loop learning is essential to gaining more insight into the causes of problems and the effective ways of solving them. Figure 17 shows single-loop learning and double-loop learning as processes initiated by a Brilliant Failure.

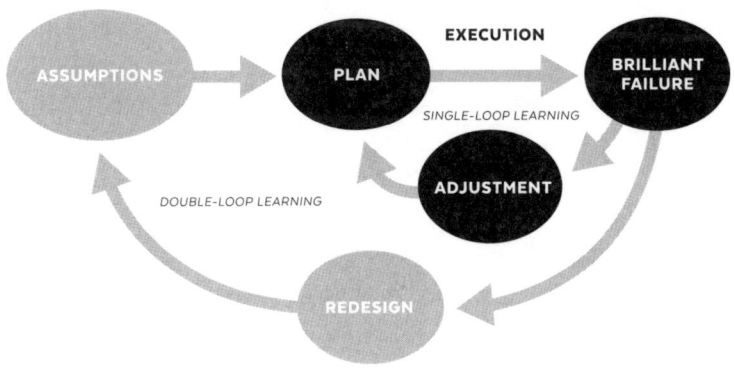

Figure 17. A Brilliant Failure as a starting point for learning processes

This image, however, insufficiently emphasizes that the learning process increases the level of knowledge. Ideally, you don't end up where you started, but at a higher level. This is why the BriFa method uses the BriFa learning spiral, which was introduced in Chapter 1. The BriFa learning spiral fits into the BriFa landscape in which learning and growth occur in a spiral, but knowledge transfer also occurs between different environments.

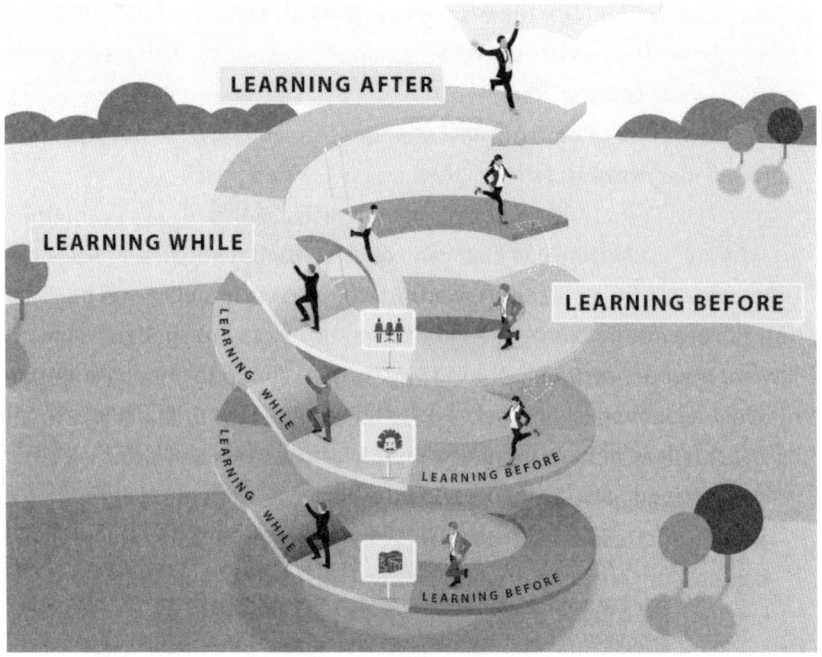

Figure 18. The BriFa landscape

The BriFa landscape is shown again in Figure 18. The various elements in this image are clear now. The spirals symbolize growth through learning. Learning can occur within a project as well, which may be a reason to start over or partially start over. This is the by-path at the third level of the spiral in the bottom left corner of the image. You can learn from past experiences; the ladder. Knowledge transfer occurs through the cables that transfer knowledge between similar situations, for example because they're characterized by the same archetype.

Although Brilliant Failures are a valuable source of new knowledge, practice has shown that this doesn't necessarily mean learning from Brilliant Failures actually occurs. There are many obstacles to both single-loop learning and double-loop learning.

Limiting factors in single-loop learning:
■ People refuse to admit or are unable to see that they're on the wrong track; they hold on to their "theory in use." Because of this, necessary adjustments aren't made or are made too late.

- People are afraid to admit that their project is failing or at risk of failure. They try to get away with this by concealing disappointing results or shifting the blame.
- There's no time to make the necessary corrections, as a result of which the project completely fails or people have to settle for a less than ideal outcome.
- There's not enough feedback from others on the process or result.

Limiting factors in double-loop learning:
- There's no time for reflecting after the activity and for making the knowledge learned explicit, transferable and/or applicable.
- There's a lack of appreciation and motivation to invest in building and maintaining the knowledge that can be applied elsewhere or later.
- Not invented here syndrome: The knowledge that was acquired in one environment is not recognized or appreciated in a different environment. People prefer to learn from their own practice.
- It's difficult to formulate the essential lessons learned in such a way that they can also be used in a different context. This is precisely why we developed the archetypes, to make it easier to turn these lessons into more transferable and universal knowledge.
- There's no appropriate infrastructure for recording and/or making accessible the lessons learned.

From organized stupidity to organized intelligence
A good example from personal experience concerns an environment with highly educatedand highly paid professionals working in a project organization. Single-loop learning wasn't the main problem here: Employees tried to successfully complete their projects in every possible way. If something didn't work, they immediately tried to come up with a different approach. Knowledge sharing within project teams usually went well, enabling everyone to perform their tasks as well as possible. These tasks primarily consisted of making a proposal, presenting it to the client, executing the project, and completing the project. But there was room for improvement at each step: Proposals could have been better formulated, the presentations could have been more attractive and appealing, and sometimes the same mistakes were made or much time was spent looking for the same

information in the execution of complex projects. If a project failed, a new project was sought as quickly as possible—the business must go on! A bonus scheme rewarded successful projects, but failed projects were not rewarded. There was no incentive for taking the time to reflect and determine which knowledge was lacking or incorrect, or to determine what did work. One of the difficulties was that many people didn't want to work for this organization very long, but saw their job as a stepping stone to a better position elsewhere. These employees weren't very sympathetic to the argument that double-loop learning is all about continuous improvement, from which the organization could benefit in the longer term. As far as they were concerned, there was no longer term.

A program designed to remove the aforementioned obstacles was set up. For example, it was determined that a project couldn't be wrapped up before an after-action review had been conducted. In addition, individual employees were assigned the responsibility of building and maintaining knowledge domains. They were rewarded for this as well. Finally, attempts were made to remove the stigma attached to failed projects and to value people not only for the results they delivered, but also for their efforts and their contributions to the collective learning process. This is how the organization battled "organized stupidity," a situation in which people together create an environment in which lack of knowledge is maintained and neither single-loop learning nor (particularly) double-loop learning is given enough space.

An interesting side question follows from the above. Imagine someone has been involved in a difficult project that ultimately failed. Another difficult project comes around. Who should be asked to participate in this project: Someone who would be doing it for the first time or the person who was involved in the failed project?

There are many ways to deal with experience gained from failed activities. A well-known example concerns Thomas Watson, the founder of IBM. One of his vice presidents developed a new product with many risks. The project ultimately failed, costing the company ten million dollars. The vice president was called into Watson's office. Convinced he'd lost his job, he asked Watson, "I guess you want my resignation?" Watson replied, "You must be kidding, we just spent ten million dollars educating you!" This reaction shows that Watson understood not only that failure is part of business life, but also that knowledge from failed projects may prove extremely valuable in the future.

Research on monkeys and brain scans has shown that the lateral frontal cortex is important in learning. It houses a number of major control functions, namely:

- temporarily storing information in the working memory;
- manipulating information (solving problems, integrating information, applying information);
- stopping on time (resisting automatic behavior, correcting behavior, responding to feedback);
- flexibility: modifying behavior based on new information.

Flexibility is the most important control function when it comes to learning ability. It requires flexibility to do something differently than you'd like to do it or would usually do it. This is the basis of learning. Learning, after all, is an interactive process between doing something, being corrected, and doing it differently. Our brains don't achieve full flexibility until we're about fifteen years old.

The Leiden Institute for Brain and Cognition (LIBC) in the Netherlands uses fMRI (functional Magnetic Resonance Imaging) to study brain activity in the frontal cortex and deeper, subcortical brain structures such as the amygdala, an almond-shaped structure involved in controlling and processing different emotions, and the corpus striatum, a structure that responds to feedback signals (Duijvenvoorde et al. (2008)). The research method is based on simple feedback learning: Participants are told they did something right or wrong and receive an external feedback signal. The question is how well people can modify their behavior, i.e., learn, in response to negative feedback or positive feedback. Participants were divided into three age categories: eight and nine, eleven to thirteen, and eighteen to twenty-five years old. The researchers investigated age-based differences in response to positive and negative feedback, focusing on activity in the various areas of the frontal cortex with their associated cognitive and emotional functions. The study showed that participants of all ages learned better based on positive feedback; that is, tasks were performed better and faster after positive feedback. However, the relative intensity of activity measured in the various brain areas did depend on age. Younger children performed considerably worse in response to negative feedback compared to older participants. This was consistent with the finding that certain brain areas in adolescents became more active in response to negative feedback, whereas these same brain areas in younger children became active in response to positive feedback. In the group of participants aged eleven to thirteen, no difference was observed between the response to positive or negative feedback. This appears to be a phase in the development of the brain during which a transition occurs in the way the learning process takes place in response to experiences or feedback.

The finding that children may perform worse after negative feedback could cautiously be interpreted to mean that their brains are not yet developed enough to learn from failure. It can be assumed that genetic predisposition is not the only factor at play here. The influence of the learning environment provided is certainly a relevant factor (memes besides genes), and research should be conducted on the effect of the development of the brain on the outcomes after correcting for the influence of social, cultural, and educational factors. More developed brains appear to be able to learn from both positive and negative experiences. Could an optimal balance be achieved by positively framing negative feedback, as happens with Brilliant Failures? Truly answering this question will require much more research, especially because the field of cognitive science and brain research is still very much developing. This definitely holds true for research on failure—the causes, consequences, and impact of interventions that influence the "climate" of failure.

Failing and Learning in the World of Science and Research
We're all familiar with the following Albert Einstein quote by now:

If we knew what we were doing,
we wouldn't call it research.

ALBERT EINSTEIN

One would expect scientists and researchers not to have any qualms about trying things out and viewing everything they encounter along the way as a learning opportunity. Research results are obviously important, but what's also important is the way these results are obtained—including the ways that led nowhere. Even negative results may be important: Disproving a hypothesis or theory provides insight into prospective developments. Furthermore, the additional knowledge gained about methods or instruments during a research project may be very valuable to others using these same tools.

An important point concerns research funding. Receiving financial support often requires a detailed research proposal to be submitted. A number of factors play a role here, the main ones of which are the relevance, originality, and feasibility of the research. The latter two factors are sometimes at odds with each other. Another factor is the candidates' track records. Having always delivered positive results in the past will improve a person's chances of receiving funding. Researchers consequently spend an enormous amount of time working on their research proposals—sometimes with a 10 percent success rate or less—and try not to emphasize the risks of their research. Another quote applies here:

It is better to aim too high and fail,
than to aim too low and succeed.

KEN ROBINSON

This leads not only to time loss and frustration, but also to research proposals that don't push the envelope.

A researcher will try their best to deliver on their promises once their research project has begun. If the proposed approach turns out not to be very promising, they usually aren't inclined to stop the project; after all, the budget has been assigned and failed research will negatively affect their reputation, so they'll keep striving to make something of it. But they'll feel increasingly bad, especially when they're being compared to other successful researchers who've published many highly cited articles in prestigious journals. Citation indexes, which keep track of how often and by whom an article has been cited, are worshipped. This leads to a peculiar form of competition: How do you score high as possible on the citation index, knowing that your score is not just determined by the quality of your research, but also by your network and the way you valorize the results of your research?

Again, quality and excellent research must be rewarded, but the knowledge necessary to get to this point—often acquired partly through failed experiences—should not be lost, and neither should the talent and passion of researchers who don't immediately make it to the top.

Nature cannot be fooled
Contribution by Bennie Mols

Joseph Weizenbaum was a thirteen-year-old Jewish boy in Berlin when his parents decided to flee from the Nazis in 1936. They left Germany behind, crossed the ocean to New York and got on a train to Detroit. After the War, Joseph Weizenbaum completed a degree in mathematics and soon felt the urge to do something useful for the world. "In that case, you should do something with computers," a colleague told him in the early fifties—a time when the number of computers in the world could be counted on the fingers of two hands.

Until then, computer programs were first written on paper and then stored on punch cards that were inserted into a computer. These programs were becoming increasingly long and complex. Weizenbaum wondered if it was possible to instead program computers by "talking" to them in natural language, the way children are taught. That way, the program would gradually become more intelligent.

Then again, what would you talk about with a computer? Realizing that computers basically know nothing about the world, Weizenbaum invented a simple script to conceal this fact: Let the computer play the role of psychotherapist, holding up a mirror to a patient by reflecting their words back to them. He came up with a way to analyze English phrases and a set of rules that would enable the computer to create answers based on key words from the phrases. He called the program ELIZA. The dialog between user and computer took place via written text only, making ELIZA the world's first chatbot.

Weizenbaum's original goal of dialog programming a computer failed. In fact, his experiment didn't teach us much about computers at all; it taught us more about people. People easily fall for the ELIZA effect, the illusion that computers understand people. This is because the human brain has a strong tendency toward anthropomorphization. We see human faces in odd-shaped clouds, think of a slow-running computer as "just having a bad day," and ascribe free will to robots that only perform preprogrammed movements.

Weizenbaum was shocked to see how readily people entrusted computers with their innermost feelings. Even his own secretary, who knew better than anyone that ELIZA was just a computer program, wanted to talk to the chatbot and once asked her boss to leave the room because she was engaged in a private conversation with ELIZA.

Finally, Weizenbaum was shocked by his peers' reactions to his work. He personally felt like he hadn't discovered anything new about computers, but most of his colleagues believed that ELIZA had paved the way to computers that can talk to and understand people. In 1970, one of Weizenbaum's colleagues at MIT told the magazine *Life*, "In from three to eight years we will have a machine with the general intelligence of an average human being."

This story reveals a more fundamental problem in the world of science and research. To secure funding, it helps to make big promises, such as "artificial intelligence will soon surpass human intelligence." Researchers who, like Weizenbaum, do a serious experiment and candidly conclude that their promise was too big or their experiment failed make it more difficult for both themselves and their colleagues to obtain research funding.

The pressure on researchers to make big promises has only increased in the last decades. For example, Dutch researchers discovered that words such as "novel" and "outstanding" currently occur in summaries of scholarly articles four times more often than they did in the seventies. In the long term, promising too much and subsequently underperforming poses a serious threat to science and research because it undermines public trust. This was perfectly put into words by Richard Feynman, Nobel Prize winner in Physics, in the conclusion of a research report on the 1986 space shuttle Challenger disaster: "For a successful technology, reality must take precedence over public relations, for nature cannot be fooled."

The above shows the importance of integrity, curiosity, and humility in the world of science and research. It's very important not only that the researchers themselves realize this, but also that the world around them learns to appreciate the value of impartial and independent thinking in the search for new knowledge, which sometimes is and often isn't applicable or directly applicable.

On useless ingenuity
Contribution by Sander Bais

We are in the midst of a social crisis. And the last straw for us to cling to, it seems, isn't religion as much as it is a sensible, independent, perhaps even rebellious mind. Oddly enough, our last hope is the revolutionary elan that lies hidden behind useless ingenuity. It seems to me a significant sign that society increasingly insists we mustn't poison the youth with useless knowledge. Contemplation is a waste of time and wasting time is a mortal sin! The road to hell is paved with circular reasoning as a symptom of doubt. Critical thinking is a form of negativity.

Pure science is like a large pantry where both crucial and useless discoveries are stored—freeze-dried, withered, sometimes even in powder form, awaiting their moment of truth. Niche knowledge is like an exotic delicacy. It's meaningless and practically worthless at first glance, until a master chef opens the pantry door, retrieves a shriveled discovery from the top shelf, puts it into an old clay pot that hasn't seen the light of day in ages, and combines it with an undefined number of other long-forgotten ingredients. New evidence has been found, or a new discovery has been made. Lo and behold, yet another concoction has been created that no one ordered or could even have come up with.

The creative thinking process keeps showing over and over again that blind pigs can find acorns. It doesn't get much more ingenious and useless than that! A tangle of completely irrational, seemingly useless arguments, a network of silly non-connections and Pollockesque idiosyncracies suddenly gives rise to a crystal-clear, sublime, irrefutable argument.

Overcoming the fear of uselessness through perseverance is something only few people manage to achieve. Indeed, it requires the persistence and courage of a blind pig trying to find an acorn. Wasn't it Newton who said, "I am like a little child playing with pebbles on the beach, whilst the great ocean of truth lies unexplored before me"? Newton? Just collecting pebbles on the beach? Such humility is inconceivable in the current era, which is replete with postgraduate courses in self-promotion. Einstein initially strongly resisted the main prediction of his theory of relativity: the solution describing the expanding universe, the very universe in which we live! Dirac was not amused when it turned out that his theory predicted something as inconceivable and literally uncalled-for as antimatter. Schrödinger reeled at the thought that his theory predicted fundamental uncertainty. These are all examples of things that initially presented as useless ingenuity, but later proved to be the driving force behind the most profound changes in our thinking. Useless the way newborns are useless, in other words.

The remarkable answer to new conformism, useless ingenuity is capable of taking a sledgehammer to a culture blinded by market forces and an obsession with usefulness.

Applying Chapter 6

1. After a project or activity, take a moment to ask yourself questions such as "What went well and why?", "What went less well and why?", and "What would I do differently next time?"

2. Talk to someone about their experience with something you're currently working on. What would you like to learn from them? Is there anything they might be able to learn from your experiences?

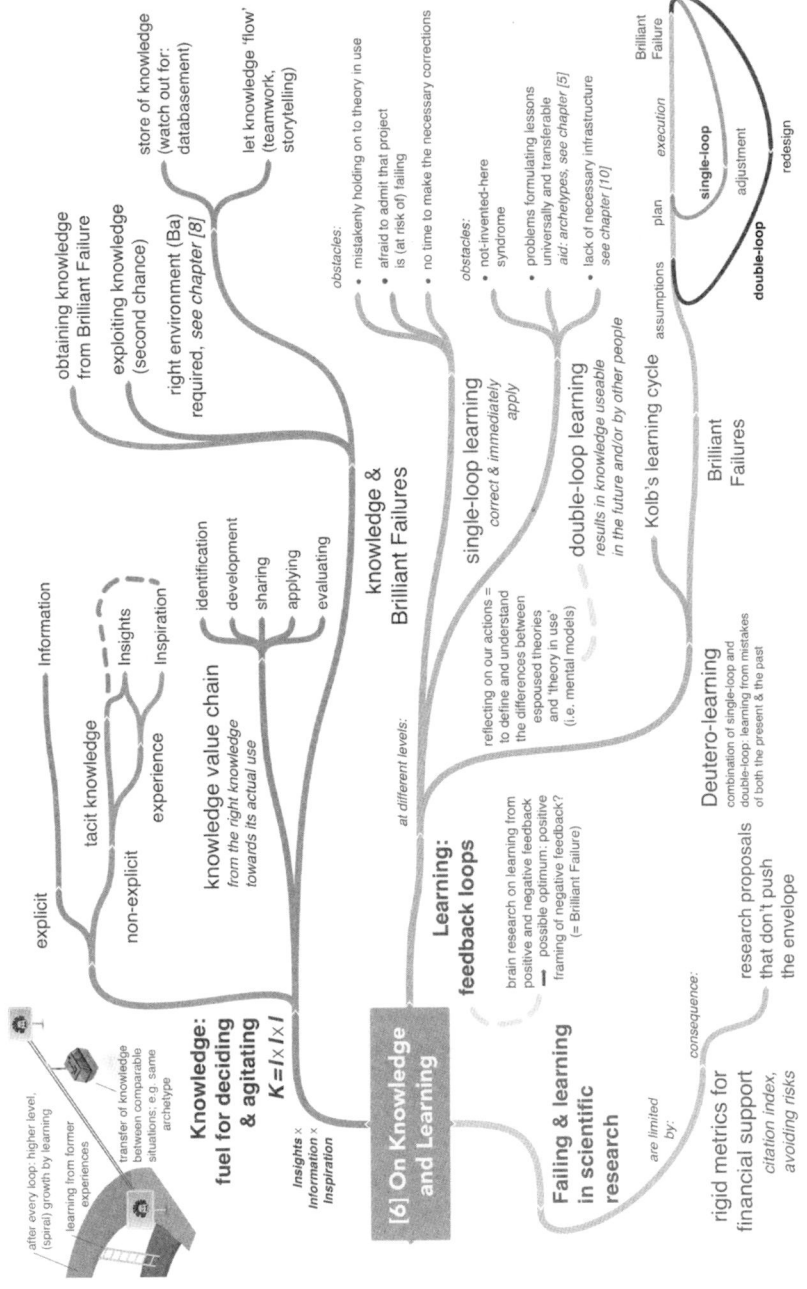

[6] On Knowledge and Learning

Knowledge: fuel for deciding & agitating

$K = I × I × I$

Insights × Information × Inspiration

- explicit — Information
- tacit knowledge
- non-explicit — experience
  - Insights
  - Inspiration
- knowledge value chain
  from the right knowledge towards its actual use
  - identification
  - development
  - sharing
  - applying
  - evaluating
- obtaining knowledge from Brilliant Failure
- exploiting knowledge (second chance)
- right environment (Ba) required, *see chapter [8]*
  - store of knowledge (watch out for: databasement)
  - let knowledge 'flow' (teamwork, storytelling)

after every loop: higher level, (spiral) growth by learning

learning from former experiences

transfer of knowledge between comparable situations; e.g. same archetype

knowledge & Brilliant Failures

at different levels:

- single-loop learning
  correct & immediately apply
  - *obstacles:*
    - mistakenly holding on to theory in use
    - afraid to admit that project is (at risk of) failing
    - no time to make the necessary corrections
- double-loop learning
  results in knowledge useable in the future and/or by other people
  - *obstacles:*
    - not-invented-here syndrome
    - problems formulating lessons universally and transferable aid: archetypes, *see chapter [5]*
    - lack of necessary infrastructure *see chapter [10]*
- Kolb's learning cycle
- Brilliant Failures

assumptions — plan — *execution* — adjustment — redesign — single-loop — double-loop — Brilliant Failure

Learning: feedback loops

- brain research on learning from positive and negative feedback — possible optimum: positive framing of negative feedback? (= Brilliant Failure)
- reflecting on our actions = to define and understand the differences between espoused theories and 'theory in use' (i.e. mental models)
- Deutero-learning
  combination of single-loop and double-loop: learning from mistakes of both the present & the past

Failing & learning in scientific research

are limited by:

- rigid metrics for financial support
  citation index, avoiding risks

consequence:

- research proposals that don't push the envelope

7. SCENARIOS: LEARNING FROM BRILLIANT FAILURES BEFORE THEY HAPPEN

When something has gone differently than we expected and/or desired, we're often tempted to say "I should've seen it coming." But that's very easy to say in hindsight. To truly be able to determine how a failure came about, it's important to put yourself in the moment when decisions were made and information either was or wasn't available. This is why it's often instructive to go back to that moment and consider what might have happened if other information or other motives had influenced the decisions made.

Alternativee History

"Alternative history" is the term used to refer to other ways events could have unfolded. An alternative history, then, is the scenario of a different outcome due to a different starting point. A well-known example of a question from alternative history concerns Adolf Hitler's limited artistic talent. Hitler tried very hard to have his paintings recognized as naïve art. To his great frustration, he didn't succeed in this. But if Hitler had been accepted into art school, would the Second World War even have taken place?

Another intriguing case is the story of Stanislav Petrov, the man who may have prevented the Third World War. Petrov was a lieutenant colonel during the Cold War period, tasked with monitoring the Soviet system for detecting incoming missile strikes from the United States. On September 26, 1983, five dots appeared on his screens, suggesting that several nuclear missiles were on their way to the Soviet Union—although they hadn't yet been detected by ground radars. Unconvinced, Petrov decided not to share his observations with his top commanders. The alert later turned out to have been a false alarm. Petrov quite possibly prevented a catastrophe by not passing it on; if he had, the Soviet military leadership may have decided to launch a retaliatory strike, which would very likely have led to a third world war. Even so, Petrov (who passed away on May 19, 2017) was not rewarded handsomely for his actions. He could count himself lucky that he wasn't punished for his inaccurate reporting of the incident, which was ultimately considered a case of system failure rather than a case of a level-headed hero preventing bad decisions from being made. Petrov later received more recognition and was awarded the Dresden Prize for preventing the Third World War.

It's interesting to consider relevant alternative histories when evaluating a chain of events, especially the influence of certain decisions on an activity or a project, after it happened. What can we learn from a different strategy than the strategy that was adopted? Which information would have made a difference? What should we have paid attention to in order to realize that things were about to wrong? Such "what if" questions can help us analyze a Brilliant Failure.

Alternative Future
This book has already discussed at length concepts such as learning and double-loop learning, that is, learning from an event or project for the benefit of later projects or activities done elsewhere or by others. But it's also possible to learn from projects that have yet to take place. An example of this approach is the so-called pre-mortem technique (see Klein (2007)), which is about imagining that a project or activity has failed and retrospectively wondering what may have caused this failure. This makes it a good instrument for group discussions aimed at increasing the chances of discovering the main risks of a project. In a pre-mortem session, the Brilliant Failure archetypes discussed in Chapter 5 can be very useful for finding and identifying risks. The pre-mortem technique is essentially a form of scenario planning: It's about considering and learning from a future that has yet to arrive, as well as from the path that led to this situation in which the "patient" has already "died." Companies such as Google also use the pre-mortem technique to create a "psychologically safe" environment (see Edmonson (1999)) in which a failure can be discussed fearlessly and openly because it hasn't actually occurred yet.

Asking the "what if" questions can help us learn from the future. This is the area of scenario planning. At its core, scenario planning is about generating alternative *futures* and exploring how our decisions turn out in those different futures. On the one hand, this can help us prevent failures by not making decisions that lead to undesirable results in most of the future scenarios considered. On the other hand, it can help us become aware of potential risks and decide whether or not we find these risks acceptable. A Brilliant Failure then occurs if we don't achieve the desired result, but aren't completely taken aback by the course of events either; it falls within the predetermined range of error, such as the maximum allowed negative impact. This may be a maximum financial loss or delay in the execution of the project, for example.

Scenarios: Learning from the Future

A Brilliant Failure is usually an outcome you did not expect and/or desire in advance—but it ended up happening anyway! Did you sufficiently take this scenario into account? "Scenario" in this context is generally defined as "a plausible, often simplified description of the way the future might unfold." The following points are worth noting here:

a. Scenarios are potential futures, often presented in a narrative or descriptive form, that create a context on the basis of which decisions can be made in the present.

b. Considering a multitude of potential future worlds will help you make better-founded decisions and create a strategy with a greater chance of success by applying the insights gained.

c. It's important to realize that scenarios don't predict the future, but rather uncover the driving forces behind changes. Understanding these driving forces will improve your ability to assess the influence of your decisions, increasing both your amount of control and your learning ability.

The History of Scenario Planning

Scenario planning as a methodology was first used in a military context. Your chances of success in a conflict are greatest when you can counter as many of your enemy's moves as possible. Just like in chess, it's not so much about predicting your opponent's next move as it is about being prepared for *any* move.

The seventies and eighties saw much theoretical and conceptual work and research on scenario planning, which usually resulted in complex academic models that are difficult to apply in practice. The real breakthrough in practical applications of scenario planning was made by oil company Shell during the 1973 oil crisis. In the fifties, Shell had already explored what would happen if oil became scarce and how the various parts of the organization such as exploration & production, refining, trading and transportcould respond to such a development. This scenario wasn't expected to happen. At the time, it was relatively easy to tap new sources of oil, so there was no technological reason to expect a global oil shortage to become a real option. Indeed, the eventual shortage wasn't caused by difficulty finding and producing oil, but by geopolitical factors. To punish Western countries for supporting Israel in the Israeli–Palestinian conflict, Arab countries greatly reduced the export of crude oil. When the oil shortage became a reality, Shell was able to act quickly on the basis of the scenario it had prepared, beating its competitors.

To be able to assess the consequences of our actions and decisions in the longer term, we have to form a corresponding picture in our minds. We can do this through:

a. Long-term thinking: We often allow ourselves to be led by spur-of-the-moment and pressing needs, but we can only determine how things will work out in the longer term by thinking far enough ahead to see new opportunities.

b. Outside-in thinking: We tend to think and reason from our own current position. We try to shape the world to our ideas and desires. By looking in from outside, we are more open to the things happening around us that may influence our activities.

c. Multiple perspectives: Taking multiple perspectives better enables us to understand our own assumptions and accept new ideas. It enables us to understand the bigger picture and the consequences of our decisions.

This allows us to distinguish the following types of developments:

■ Possible: These are developments that *could* occur, not taking probability into account. Afterward, we can only determine that the development in question either did or didn't occur. In other words, this is future knowledge that is not yet available.

■ Plausible: These kinds of developments may occur, but they may just as likely not occur. This two-sided probability can be determined on the basis of knowledge that is available right now, such as calculations or past experiences.

■ Probable: Some developments are likely to occur, which can be determined in advance. These kinds of developments can usually be identified by analyzing current trends and extrapolating from these changes.

■ Desired: Tread carefully here! Our preferences for certain future scenarios may lead us to assign greater probability to the corresponding developments than can realistically be justified. As a result, we become blinded and only see the consequences of our decisions in the world we'd like to create.

Let's briefly return to the example of going on vacation. Imagine you chose Norway as your destination. In addition to being a beautiful country, Norway has another distinctive feature: the weather is relatively unpredictable. Weather is often a relevant factor in choosing a vacation destination. A plausible development in this scenario would be a period of bad weather with rain and low temperatures, although fine summer weather is certainly a possibility as well.

Armed with this information, you can start developing scenarios and use them to decide, for example, what to bring (particularly clothing) and how to spend your time, taking into account your travel companions' wishes and demands.

Working with scenarios

Below is a step-by-step description of a scenario-planning exercise.

1. Decide what the exercise about.
   a. Which burning question are you trying to answer or problem are you trying to solve, e.g. how much money to invest, what to pack for vacation, whether or not to propose to your partner, whether or not to drop out of university to focus on your sports career, what PhD topic to choose…?
   b. Focus primarily on decisions you have to make right now.
   c. Consider a longer time horizon than you usually would. Your goal is to discover how your decisions will turn out over a longer period than you would normally be able to plan for.
   d. Keep an open mind; postpone thoughts like "That probably won't happen anyway."
   e. Ask yourself whether you'll later be in the same position you are in now and how you might look back on your decisions.
2. Explore both the internal and the external environment to identify potential areas of change that may influence the topic of your scenario-planning exercise. For example, economic change may affect your financial position, you may lose your job, fall in love…. again, etc.
3. Select the underlying drivers of change and determine their levels of uncertainty:
   a. *Low uncertainty* means that we are reasonably sure something will either occur, not occur, or occur in a predictable manner. Consider, for example, the chance of frost in Hawaii in the summer. This has a low level of uncertainty; you're quite sure it won't happen. We often say that something is very risky when we mean there's a good chance it won't work out. In other words, it actually has a low level of uncertainty.
   b. *High uncertainty* indicates that we don't know whether something will occur, not occur, or occur in an unpredictable manner. Some

people's behavior is unpredictable, as is the behavior of large groups of customers. Political decisions, technological developments, and the weather in countries such as the Netherlands are also relatively unpredictable, but may be relevant to the issue at hand. Brilliant Failures are often caused by high levels of uncertainty.

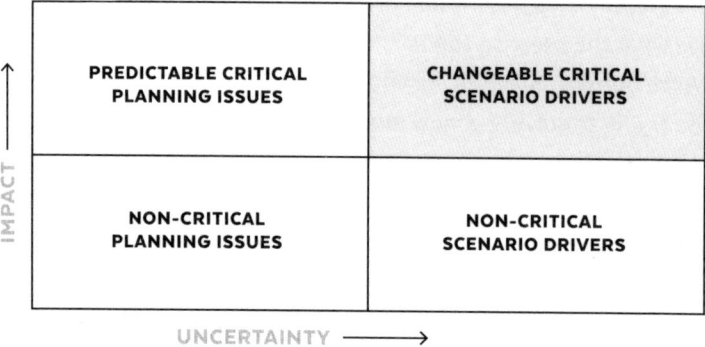

Figure 19. Critical scenario drivers

4. Construct the scenario matrix. In a scenario matrix, you not only indicate which factors have a high, low, or moderate level of uncertainty, but also how important these factors are to your activities. It will probably suffice to just monitor factors with a low level of uncertainty, although vigilance is always necessary. If a factor is very important, you'll need to correctly include it in your scenarios no matter what, or else a not-so-brilliant failure may be lying in wait. The most interesting combination from the perspective of scenario planning are those factors that are both highly uncertain and greatly affect the end result at the same time. In some markets, offering a product or introducing a new product comes with the risk of changing customer values affecting the valuation of your product. For example, incidents such as bombings often cause tourism industries to collapse (usually temporarily), affecting travel agencies offering vacations to unstable regions.

5. Further develop the scenarios. This step involves turning the scenarios into "stories," whether textually, visually, or using any other form of communication. Scenarios are generally presented in a narrative form.

It's not about whether a scenario becomes a reality; it's more about how your decisions would turn out in the future world in question. Look around in this potential future and learn from what you see and how your decisions manifest themselves here. Scenarios must be internally consistent, that is, they must follow logically from the analyses you made based on factors that are relevant and uncertain, but also correctly include relevant and probable factors.

6. Now consider the strategic implications of the scenarios. It's not so much about the scenarios themselves as it is about thinking freely and being open to things that might happen. The mere act of preparing scenarios is already an activity that improves your ability to see risks and determine whether they are acceptable:

   a. It gives you a better overview of what options will eventually be available.

   b. It encourages you to engage in long-term thinking and outside-in thinking.

   c. It helps you become more conscious of your surroundings. By creating a framework based on your own thoughts and decisions, you become more aware of certain signals and suddenly see options and opportunities you didn't see before.

   d. It makes you more aware of the risks and how to deal with them.

   e. It provides you with more insight into the influence of your decisions in various future worlds. Is your approach appropriate in each scenario or do you have to hope for a specific scenario to eventually become a reality?

   f. What can you influence in order to increase your chances of success? For example, can you still change your decision, prevent a scenario from becoming a reality, or come up with a way to reduce the impact of a negative outcome?

   g. Are there any early signals you can or should pick up that indicate which scenario is becoming a reality?

   h. How will you incorporate the learning experiences you gained from this exercise into your action plan?

The core message in applying scenario planning to Failing Brilliantly is that *failure is an option*. Identifying all certainties and uncertainties and combining them with their relevance will help improve your understanding of potential failures, their causes, and what you can do to pick up signals that indicate things are going differently than expected as early as possible. Having scenarios prepared will allow you to respond faster and reduce negative consequences as much as possible by acting quickly and correctly.

It may be useful to engage in a scenario-planning exercise when discussing and evaluating a project, activity or enterprise after it happened, turning back time to the moments when crucial decisions were made. This way, you'll see not only reality as it eventually turned out, but also alternative realities in which the uncertainties—whether they were known in advance or became apparent at a later time—could have led to very different results. This form of learning can not only provide more insight into the project at hand, but also help you in similar future projects by improving your ability to identify key decision-making moments and determine the potential influence of a complex and changeable environment on the eventual result of the decisions that were made and the actions that were taken.

The inevitable cultural revolution
Contribution by Wim de Ridder

The intention
The field of future studies is rife with Brilliant Failures. After all, predictions about new technologies, new products and a new society are by definition explorations of an unknown world. Let's consider an example.

Twenty years ago saw the rise of the Internet, which soon proved to be a revolutionary development. As science journalist Margaret Wertheim put it, "All around us cyberspace explodes into being with the exponential force of its own big bang." Parallels were drawn with the creation of the universe approximately fifteen billion years ago. Derrick de Kerckhove, the then director of the McLuhan Program in Culture & Technology at the University of Toronto, saw a new world arise alongside the physical and mental space in which we live. Geneticist Richard Dawkins attracted attention by arguing for a prominent place for memes, "gene-like properties of certain ideas that reproduce, colonize niches, and adapt to the environment of a society's collective mind." All this set the scene for the 1998 anniversary book of the Society and Enterprise Foundation (SMO), where I was serving as director at the time.

The approach
No less than 38 authors shared their views on the consequences of the rise of the Internet. The anniversary book came with *The New Little Red Book*, a summary comparing quotes from Chinese communist leader Mao Zedong to quotes from this book, which described a radically different world. The highlight was the anniversary celebration itself with a performance of the play *The Inevitable Cultural Revolution*, directed by acclaimed Dutch theater director Johan Simons. In this play, Johan Simons—a firm believer in the inevitable cultural revolution—anticipated a time when hierarchical relationships in companies have been replaced with self-managing organizations.

The result
The play showed entrepreneurs climbing the social ladder and clashing with a glass ceiling symbolizing the limits of their power. *The Inevitable Cultural Revolution* also determined the future of the SMO; the leading, established companies that had set up this corporate think tank in the memorable year 1968 had no affinity with the future presented here and parted ways with the SMO. It was a Brilliant Failure.

The lessons learned

This time also saw the rise of so-called Internet companies. The CEOs of the five largest IT companies in 2000 had two things in common: All of them had studied at Harvard and none of them had completed their studies. Established companies were not in touch with digital development, so there was little to no competition. In 2018, these IT companies are all still top stock market companies with few competitors. Apple, for example, is approaching a one trillion-dollar market cap and has a cash reserve of over 250 billion dollars. It can buy anything.

We live in a time of "digital Darwinism," the term used to refer to the fact that digital technology has much more to offer than most people and companies realize. And it's only getting worse: Digital technology is developing at an exponential rate. Many companies now fear that their business will be taken over by disruptors, whose digital processes make them more profitable. More and more companies are learning the hard way that "if you're not at the table, you're on the menu" and taking precautions. They go out in search of the formula for success used by large IT companies and discover what the literature refers to as an MTP, a Massively Transformative Purpose.

Renowned companies such as AkzoNobel and Unilever can no longer decide on their own independence. The rise of blockchain technology will bring us face to face with powerful self-managing organizations, as predicted in *The Inevitable Cultural Revolution*. There are currently so many disruptive developments that naming facts is more effective than considering the near future. Futurists are increasingly asked to supervise the digital transformation of companies. A well-thought-out vision of the inevitable cultural revolution is less appreciated, even now that this knowledge is essential to be successful.

War-Gaming: Failing Brilliantly in the Future

There are sectors in which failure and safety are directly linked at the life-and-death level. The military context is a clear example of this. Acts of war, peacekeeping missions, and major military rescue operations are all characterized by a high level of complexity and the associated (safety) risks. Military environments consequently contain various elements that improve learning ability. As previously mentioned, scenario planning was first used in a military context; so was After Action Review, a systematic tool for analyzing what happened, what went well, and what could have gone better. But the world is changing dramatically, as are its defense-related aspects. Conflicts change in nature, for example because of modern weaponry and the proliferation thereof. A new component has now been added: cyberwar, potentially creating a whole new battlefield with possibly even greater interdependencies and therefore complexity.

Despite great efforts, things sometimes go wrong—sometimes horribly wrong. An example of this is the 1995 Srebrenica massacre during the Bosnian War, where Dutch soldiers acting as UN peacekeepers failed to protect Muslim refugees in a UN-designated safe zone. This tragedy, which deeply affected Dutch society, provides a clear opportunity for system-level learning. One can only hope this learning opportunity will be taken, and one can only wish it hadn't come at such a terribly high price.

Failing and war-gaming in a military environment
Contribution by Hans Steensma and Erik Elgersma

Making mistakes is a must
Imagine a company or organization whose leadership actively encourages its employees to make mistakes. What kind of organization would do that? Most organizations want to grow, or at least safeguard their continuity. This goal seems incompatible with making mistakes. Mistakes cost money, disappoint the customer, cause confusion... How could an organization possibly encourage this? Can making mistakes

really help organizations grow? You may be wondering how. The answer to this question is actually not at all surprising. Making minor mistakes now will enable you to anticipate and prevent serious mistakes later. Letting people make manageable mistakes allows them to rapidly develop skills, preparing the organization to respond to an uncertain future.

Take the United States Marine Corps. It was established 243 years ago in 1775, making it an excellent example of continuity. What would the Commandant of the Marine Corps find important to share with his subordinates so they can respond to the chaos and complexity of the battlefield? He (no she yet) is very clear about this, encouraging Marines to bring out the best in themselves and the Corps by learning: "You will have my commitment that we will operate in a decentralized manner that capitalizes on the leadership, initiative, intellect, aggressiveness, and innovativeness of Marines at all levels (...). Fully leveraging the talent and ability of every Marine is a critical component of our warfighting culture. I realize that this method will sometimes lead to imperfect results, but leaders at all levels must be willing to accept mistakes as part of the learning process."

Failing brilliantly in a practice environment
Soldiers spend a lot of time training and practicing. They do this to get better at what they have to do and have to be able to do, but also to make controlled mistakes and experiment with new methods and behaviors.

Military exercises may take place on military training grounds, away from the normal world and prying eyes. These are places for practicing tactics and procedures step by step, where resistance can be simulated. It's like staged role play, with soldiers as players reenacting their own actions. Trying out things you wouldn't be able to do in real life without consequences provides a great opportunity for learning. In a way, then, training or practicing can partly be defined as Failing Brilliantly in an organized way. Making mistakes is not incidental or secondary, but a preconceived goal.

Practice in the form of a game
So-called war games are deliberately created environments as well. A war game is essentially a virtual environment in which the making and testing of operation plans can be practiced. It's not just about the game, but mainly about the players. Their decisions and their ability to reason from someone else's perspective make it possible to create scenarios that might occur. The ability to reason from another perspective is crucial in preparing for potential resistance or support. Asking the right questions, using knowledge and experience to the fullest extent, daring to combine insights, and fiercely defending action plans are essential skills that can be developed by playing war games. As a war game expert recently put it, "Experts predict what should happen, role play predicts what will happen."

Practicing battles is equally useful and necessary for companies in these ever-changing markets. There are countless similarities between the military context and the business context. War gaming in a business context allows teams to experience their market competitor's opportunities and threats and subsequently use these experiences to generate plans with a higher probability of success. "The more you sweat in training, the less you bleed in combat" applies in a business context, too—except you'll be bleeding cash instead of blood. War games can thus be used to create a library of "memories of the possible future," if you will, which you can consult as a travel guide when the war game scenario presents itself in said future.

Applying Chapter 7

1. Is there anything on your mind right now? For example, are you thinking about buying a house, changing jobs, enrolling in a course, going on vacation, visiting the in-laws...? Develop scenarios by considering factors that may influence the outcome but are outside your sphere of influence, such as economic change, your health, the weather in your destination, your parents-in-laws' moods, or employment trends. How do you deal with scenarios containing failure?

2. Would your life be much more appealing if everything went according to plan?

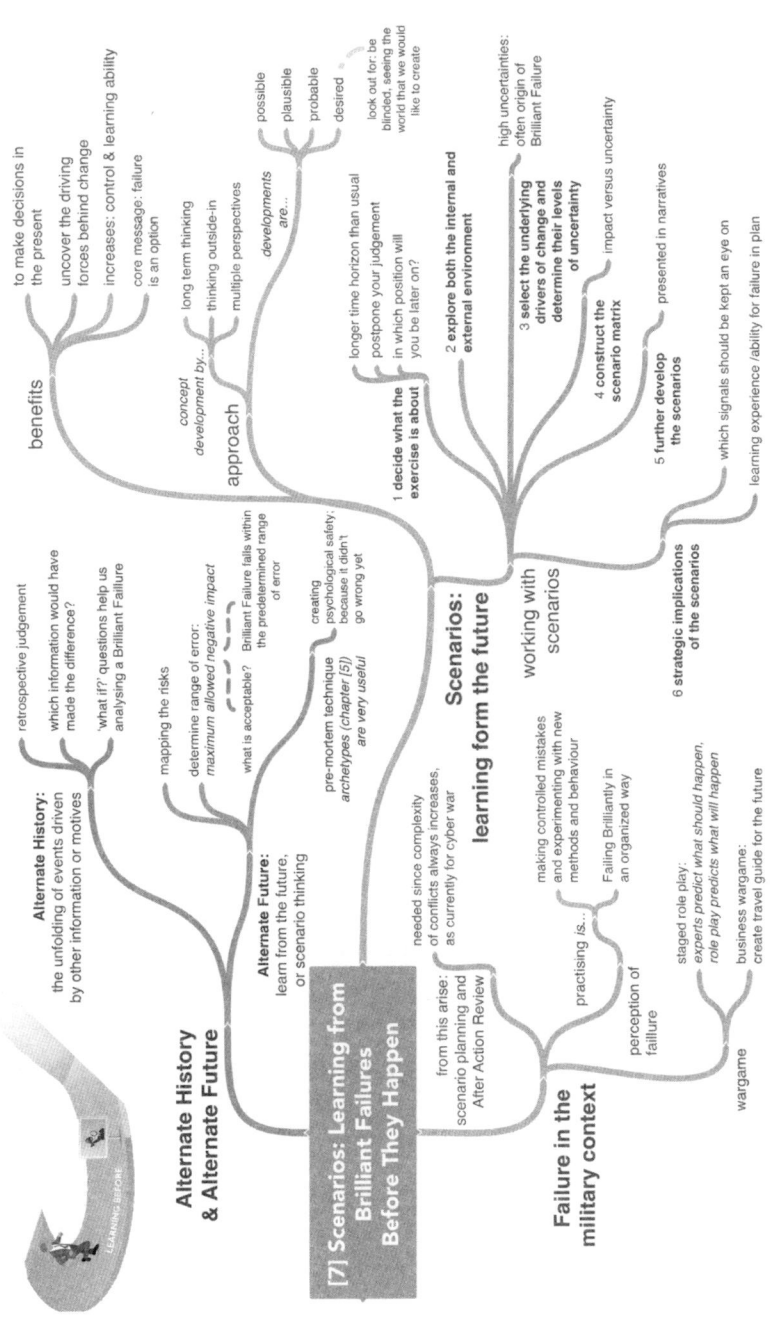

Alternate History & Alternate Future

Alternate History:
the unfolding of events driven by other information or motives

- retrospective judgement
- which information would have made the difference?
- 'what if?' questions help us analysing a Brilliant Failure

mapping the risks

Alternate Future:
learn from the future, or scenario thinking

- determine range of error: *maximum allowed negative impact*
- what is acceptable? — Brilliant Failure fails within the predetermined range of error
- pre-mortem technique *archetypes (chapter [5]) are very useful*
- creating psychological safety, because it didn't go wrong yet

[7] Scenarios: Learning from Brilliant Failures Before They Happen

from this arise: scenario planning and After Action Review

practising is...
- making controlled mistakes and experimenting with new methods and behaviour
- Failing Brilliantly in an organized way

perception of failure

Failure in the military context

needed since complexity of conflicts always increases, as currently for cyber war

staged role play:
experts predict *what should happen,* role play predicts *what will happen*

business wargame:
create travel guide for the future

wargame

Scenarios: learning form the future

working with scenarios

benefits
- to make decisions in the present
- uncover the driving forces behind change
- increases: control & learning ability
- core message: failure is an option

concept development by...
- long term thinking
- thinking outside-in
- multiple perspectives

approach
developments are...
- possible
- plausible
- probable
- desired — look out for: be blinded, seeing the world that we would like to create

1 decide what the exercise is about
- longer time horizon than usual
- postpone your judgement in which position will you be later on?

2 explore both the internal and external environment

3 select the underlying drivers of change and determine their levels of uncertainty
- high uncertainties: often origin of Brilliant Failure
- impact versus uncertainty

4 construct the scenario matrix
- presented in narratives

5 further develop the scenarios
- which signals should be kept an eye on
- learning experience /ability for failure in plan

6 strategic implications of the scenarios

8. THE IMPORTANCE OF A SAFE ENVIRONMENT

As mentioned previously, it's important to create a positive image of Brilliant Failures. People should be able to try, fail, and learn without fear. A positive environment arises when people themselves, as well as managers, friends, family members, customers, employees, members of the press, etc., are open to well-intentioned attempts and the resulting outcomes and key learning points. Encouraging "controlled failure" helps organizations improve their approach to issues such as innovation, safety, and improvement management. This does, however, require the stigma of failure to be removed.

The Influence of the Environment

People are often hesitant to be the first to "come clean" in environments where admitting to failure doesn't feel safe.

There's an element of the so-called prisoner's dilemma at play here. This is a concept from game theory in which two players both possess incriminating information, for example because they committed armed robbery together. The prosecutor is trying to get them to turn on each other by offering them a deal in exchange for a confession. The deal is as follows: If A testifies against B, A gets off scot-free and B receives a long prison sentence. If B testifies against A, B gets off scot-free and A receives a long prison sentence. If they both testify against each other, both receive short prison sentences. If neither A nor B testifies, both are fined for criminal possession of a weapon, as the rest of the charges cannot be substantiated. What will they do? The best option for both players is to remain silent and accept the fine. This way, neither of them will go to jail. But do they trust each other? For each player individually, it's better to confess quickly and be rewarded for their cooperation—which, of course, has many negative consequences for the other player.

In a way, the reverse applies to "confessing" to a Brilliant Failure. Is it a good idea to be the first to speak up about a potentially Brilliant Failure and the lessons you learned? What if having caused or been involved in a failure has negative consequences for you after all? What if no one else speaks up, causing knowledge to get lost and fear of failure to remain in place? A person's decision to speak up is largely determined by the anticipated response of their environment. The "system" in which you live and work, in other words, greatly influences your everyday actions, utterances, and value judgments. Consequently, it also influences the difference between success and failure.

Essentially, this entire book is primarily about behavior. A person's behavior depends on their characteristics and history, e.g. genetic profile, upbringing, education. These are intrinsic factors, but people are also exposed to extrinsic factors. The combination of intrinsic and extrinsic factors ultimately determines someone's behavior and the decisions they make. To better describe the conditions under which experimentation and learning can thrive, it's useful to elaborate on the concept of "environment." We'll adhere to the following definition of environment from the American Heritage© Science Dictionary: "All of the biotic and abiotic factors that act on an organism, population or ecological community and influence its survival and development. Biotic factors include the organisms themselves, their food and their interactions. Abiotic factors include such items as sunlight, soil, air, water, climate, and pollution. Organisms respond to changes in their environment by evolutionary adaptations in form and behavior."

In the present context, we're concerned with interactions with the environment that influence the behavior of people and organizations. These interactions occur in four different "spaces":

1. The social/cultural space. We primarily draw positive energy from connecting with and getting feedback from others. An important aspect of the social space is accepting each other, especially when it comes to giving each other room to make mistakes. In complex environments, progress cannot be forced or predicted; the outcome of a process is by definition uncertain. Acceptance of the outcome is of great importance. People fare better in environments that provide encouragement and positive feedback.

2. The process/organizational space. This space is determined by the agreements that have been made, including incentives, the organizational form, and legislation and regulation. People often experience this part of an environment as imposed from above. The process space can have a powerful influence on behavior. It may conflict with people's needs or beliefs and create negative feelings, for example in cases of overregulation or excessive bureaucracy.

3. The virtual/digital space. IT developments have undoubtedly contributed greatly to new opportunities for creating, sharing, and using intellectual capital. Distance is no longer a barrier and everyone and everything can be connected nowadays. This has particularly led to the development of social networks, which make knowledge discovery possible. A side note: Before investing heavily in new technology, it's important to realize that the organization must also change. If this doesn't happen, you'll encounter the aforementioned "law" of NT + OO = EOO: New Technology in Old Organizations results in Expensive Old Organizations.

4. The physical/real space. In addition to the importance of the virtual space, various studies have pointed out the importance of a suitable physical space. Such a space is open, encourages chance encounters, and inspires through a combination of interior design, programming, and hospitality. Colors, smells, shapes, temperature, nature, and art are

examples of aspects of the physical environment that may influence the emotional state of the people in it.

Biomimicry: What We Can Learn from Nature

Nature is a great source of inspiration in many areas. Design principles can be applied to the design of products, services, organizations, and even society itself. In her book *Biomimicry* (1998), Janine Benyus describes how nature has inspired numerous innovations. Velcro, for example, was invented by a Swiss engineer named George de Mestral, who noticed cockleburs clinging stubbornly to his pants and his dog's coat on a hike.

Nature also contains many Brilliant Failures. Species that cannot adapt to changing circumstances go extinct; random mutations result in superior species; animals accidentally discover how something works and manage to pass this knowledge on to other members of their species; diseases threaten the existence of certain species in ecosystems, which in turn threatens the existence of the ecosystems themselves, and so on. The sum of all this is the evolutionary process by which nature attempts to secure the future of species and ecosystems. Learning from Brilliant Failures is a core process in this.

Charles Leadbeater (2000) wrote an article in which he applies the principle of biomimicry to organizational climates for innovation. Natural ecosystems are evolving systems; the article compares organizations to ecosystems, both of which must adapt to changing circumstances. Nature explicitly learns from experimentation and variation, preserving what works and letting what fails go extinct. This inspired Leadbeater to use evolution as a metaphor for innovation. He distinguishes nine factors that influence the adaptability of natural ecosystems, subsequently projecting them onto corresponding conditions within organizations. These nine principles are:

1. Diversity. Random genetic mutation is an important mechanism for biological diversity. Innovative companies create various portfolios of ideas and knowledge sources. They're able to actively use diversity within and outside the organization. They look for fresh blood to gain access to new ideas and knowledge.

2. Selection. More successful genetic mutations are identified through natural selection. Many organizations, however, struggle with selecting the right projects and abandoning less promising initiatives. Their decision criteria are often unclear or they tend to stick with "what's always worked."

3. Perpetuation. Successful species are able to reproduce and spread their genetic material. Innovative companies are able to share their knowledge and ideas and embed them in organizational processes and routines while simultaneously using them in new products and services for their customers.

4. Co-evolution. Species can only survive if they're fit for their environment. Organizations must similarly co-evolve with their environment (customers, partners, competitors, other stakeholders) to be able to do business, attract employees, and develop new markets in the longer term.

5. Unlearning. Species that cling to their habits and cannot adapt will go extinct when the demands of their environment change. Many organizations find it difficult to part ways with existing (and often previously successful) habits, relationships and knowledge, even if it's clear that these cannot be further developed. Young people's ideas often lose out to existing organizational wisdom and experience.

6. Disruption. Biological "explosions," such as the emergence of multicellular organisms more than half a billion years ago, occur in environments in transition. Organizations that know how to respond to radical changes in their environment are well positioned to co-evolve and enter a new period of prosperity.

7. Simplicity. Surviving species often exhibit a certain kind of simplicity. Unnecessary complexity stands in the way of successful reproduction and/or dispersal. Similarly, progress in organizations is often impeded by overly complicated processes and procedures and by bureaucracy sucking energy from new plans and initiatives. Successful organizations, by contrast, adhere to clear goals and values. They give their employees many responsibilities to allow innovation and entrepreneurship to grow and flourish.

8. Spare capacity. Evolution is largely based on trial and error, with species appearing and then disappearing again if found unfit. Darwin's mechanism thus involves a considerable amount of spare capacity. Organizations, especially in times of crisis, tend to suffer from "corporate anorexia": Nothing is allowed to fail, everything must be under control, and plans have to account for everything. This may affect opportunities for innovation and entrepreneurship.

9. Timing. Sometimes species with seemingly promising genetic material are ultimately unsuccessful because their timing was off and their changing circumstances were unfavorable to their reproduction and/or dispersal at the critical moment. Similarly, developments within or outside organizations often fail because they came either too late or too early(!). Many innovations come at a time when the market is still insufficiently capable of recognizing or seizing the opportunities, or when too many competing developments have reached the market at the same time.

The nine principles of evolutionary innovation can easily be linked directly to the factors that foster an environment for sensibly dealing with Brilliant Failures. This is because the metaphor of evolving systems is also an excellent metaphor for environments in which experimentation and learning takes place. In both contexts, learning processes—particularly double-loop learning processes—are extremely important. And just like in nature, the lessons learned are only meaningful when put into practice.

The central question of this book can thus be formulated as follows:

Why do we find it so difficult to accept the natural process
of making mistakes and learning from failure?

The BriFa method uses the nine principles of evolutionary innovation to identify strengths and weaknesses of a favorable climate for experimentation and learning.

Serious Optimism

Together with the Institute of Brilliant Failures we've introduced the concept of "Serious Optimism," which involves a number of environmental factors that influence the creation of positive energy. Positive energy helps people and organizations be more able and motivated to be entrepreneurial and open to experiences that may be valuable to themselves and others with whom the lessons learned can be shared.

Many people believe that positive thinking increases their chances of success. Under certain conditions, optimism can indeed help people achieve their goals. Research has shown that having a positive or negative view of the world affects people's behavior and is often the determining factor in the decision to either continue or give up (Scheier & Carver, 1993). One example of such research is an article on the significance of positive psychology in the classroom (Seligman et al., 2009). It can be stated that, under certain conditions, more optimistic people tend to work harder to achieve their goals in the face of setbacks (Strack, Carver & Blaney, 1987).

This conclusion about the benefits of optimism is as obvious as it is welcome. Some reservation is necessary, though, as life is often more complicated than we'd like it to be. Various studies point to the mixed effect of optimism on performance. On the one hand, optimism is seen as a characteristic of successful entrepreneurs (Crane & Crane, 2007) and has a positive effect on organizational performance, along with hope, resilience and efficacy (Luthans, Avolio, Avey, & Norman, 2007; Luthans & Youssef, 2004). On the other hand, entrepreneurs' optimism can also have a negative effect on the performance of new ventures (Hmieleski & Baron, 2009). This occurs when misplaced optimism, based on irrational estimates, leads to risky decisions. It's therefore important to find the right balance between optimism and realism. This balance has been called "realistic optimism" (Peterson, 2000; Schneider, 2001).

"Serious Optimism" is a related term referring to a collection of well-thought-out interventions that lead to realistic optimism, linked to performance enhancement. It can help us avoid lapsing into naive positivity—or positive naivety. Wandering onto the highway with your eyes closed is optimistic, but not very sensible. "Serious," then, here applies to both the optimism and the realism. This is in line with the essence of dealing with Brilliant Failures and our positive framing of experimentation and learning.

In Norwegian, Serious Optimism translates to *Seriøs Oppmuntring*. The history of this term dates back to 1999, to the impending closure of a local school because of a student shortage in the village Næroset, between Hamar and Lillehammer. The local community decided to protest against the closure in various positive and playful ways, including entering into an international friendship pact with Kuala Lumpur, establishing a museum for discarded Christmas trees (to which the Prime Minister of Norway contributed), and organizing many activities aimed at social cohesion. Ultimately, the amount of goodwill and attention generated was so great that the village is now known as "Lucky Næroset" and the school is still open.

Enthusiasm is an important state of mind for achieving goals with a positive attitude. But what makes us enthusiastic? Research at the Köln International School of Design in Cologne identified nine universal factors (Mager, 2011):

1. Relief: Experiencing that problems are being solved or time is being saved or receiving help in making difficult decisions;
2. Flexibility: Having our environment adapt to us instead of always having to adapt to organizations, processes, products, culture, etc.;
3. Generosity: Receiving more than we thought we would;
4. Solidarity: Feeling like someone else truly understand us, takes into account our circumstances, and thinks ahead with and for us;
5. Success: Achieving personal success through a relationship with something or someone, partly by making use of available services and products;
6. Beauty: Being moved by something beautiful or aesthetically pleasing;
7. Exclusiveness: Getting or experiencing something that not everyone gets to have or experience, which makes us feel "chosen";
8. Connectedness: Discovering that something or someone we want to associate with is a good fit for us;
9. Authenticity: Feeling like something is real and genuine, transparent and sincere.

Share your uplifting story: Apptimism

The power of stories is important in transferring knowledge and enthusing people. Storytelling has long proven to be an effective method of saving and sharing knowledge within communities. It was recently rediscovered as a management tool to support various processes, such as marketing, innovation, and reorganization. The Institute of Serious Optimism has also developed a storytelling tool for sharing "apptimisms," stories that inspire optimism. The app is available for download in all app stores. You can use your smart phone to take a picture of the uplifting situation, further describing it using a semi-formatted text (see Figure 20).

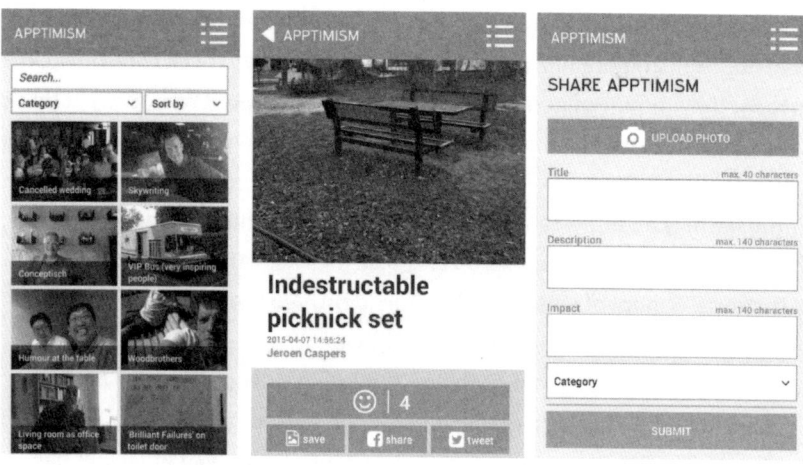

Figure 20. "Apptimism," a storytelling tool for Serious Optimism

Although the concept of Serious Optimism is still in its infancy, the approach seems to be an appropriate new way to gain insights that may lead to a more conscious use of positive energy in developing organizations and communities. The importance of this kind of thinking with regard to dealing with Brilliant Failures is an open, positive attitude toward activities whose outcome is uncertain and appreciation of the attempt and the lessons that can be learned from it. In fact, everyone should have the right to Fail Brilliantly! This is why we've written the following amendment to the Universal Declaration of Human Rights:

Universal Declaration of the Right to Fail Brilliantly

Preamble

Whereas there is a common ambition to succeed and good preparation, a project and/or activity may turn out differently than planned or desired;

Whereas a "Brilliant Failure" is an attempt to create value whose originally intended result wasn't achieved, even though no avoidable or culpable mistakes were made; lessons were learned and learning experiences are being shared;

Whereas recognizing the right to Fail Brilliantly is a basis for psychological safety and personal and organizational evolution, and therefore a basis for the ability to forgive, put into perspective, and learn from failed attempts, not only at an individual but also at the organizational level;

Now, therefore, the Institute of Brilliant Failures proclaims that every individual and every organization, keeping this Declaration constantly in mind, shall strive to promote respect for these rights and freedoms and by progressive measures to secure their universal and effective recognition and observance:

ARTICLE 1

Every person has the right to have their failed attempts be forgiven and put into perspective and to learn from them.

ARTICLE 2

Every person in every layer of an organization or society has the Right to Fail Brilliantly.

ARTICLE 3

You have the right to psychological safety and personal evolution.

ARTICLE 4

You have the right to try.

ARTICLE 5

You have the right to protection of your reputation.

The month-of-birth effect

As it stands, the right to fail is certainly not an inherent right. A person may even be more likely to fail due to organized stupidity in their environment and subsequently not get a second chance to achieve their goal. A glaring example of this is the so-called "month-of-birth effect," where a person's chances of success are influenced by their date of birth. In many youth sports programs, for example, children are divided into teams based on the year they were born. This means that a child born in January falls into the same age category as a child born in December of the same year. But in young children, this difference of almost a year may be very significant. The older child will probably be both mentally and physically more mature, performing better as a result. They'll stand out, be praised, feel more confident, and may even be advanced to a higher-level team, allowing them to improve, and so on and so forth. This effect has been shown to continue into adulthood. For example, research has found that there are more than twice as many professional soccer players in the Netherlands who were born in January compared to professional soccer players born in December.

The situation is just as bad in education. In the Dutch secondary education system, children are divided not just by age, but also by ability; they receive four, five, or six years of secondary education, depending on the level they're in. The cut-off date for starting school in the Netherlands is usually October 1st. Children born on or after October 1st start school later than children born before October 1st. This has also been shown to have an effect. Children born between October and December are 30 percent more likely to take the highest level of secondary education than children born between July and September. Isn't that crazy? I was recently at the school one of my children attends for an information session on the transition from the first to the second year of secondary education. They informed us that the requirements were very strict and children who failed to meet them would be shipped off to a lower level of education. ("Shipped off" isn't the term they used, but they might as well have.) We were told that many children would meet this fate, often because they're supposedly not yet ready for a higher level of education. From this, we can conclude that they may fail not so much because of a lack of talent, but simply because they haven't matured enough yet. I asked whether it wouldn't make sense to give children who were still too young a second chance. Everyone develops at their own rate, after all, and the month-of-birth effect might be playing a role here as well. Certainly not, they said; rules are rules. Ship 'em off! This shows that, in unfavorable environments, people can fail without a right to a second chance. I say organized and malignant stupidity is a violation of the Universal Declaration of the Right to Fail! I find it incomprehensible that not even children are afforded this human right.

Applying Chapter 8

1. Write your own apptimism. After going to the website www.apptimism.eu and creating an account, you can use "share apptimism" or scan the QR code on the right to share your apptimisms. Do this regularly and share your apptimisms with others!

2. When would you appreciate a second chance? What did you learn from your first attempt, what would you have done differently and what would help you to become succesful in your second attempt?

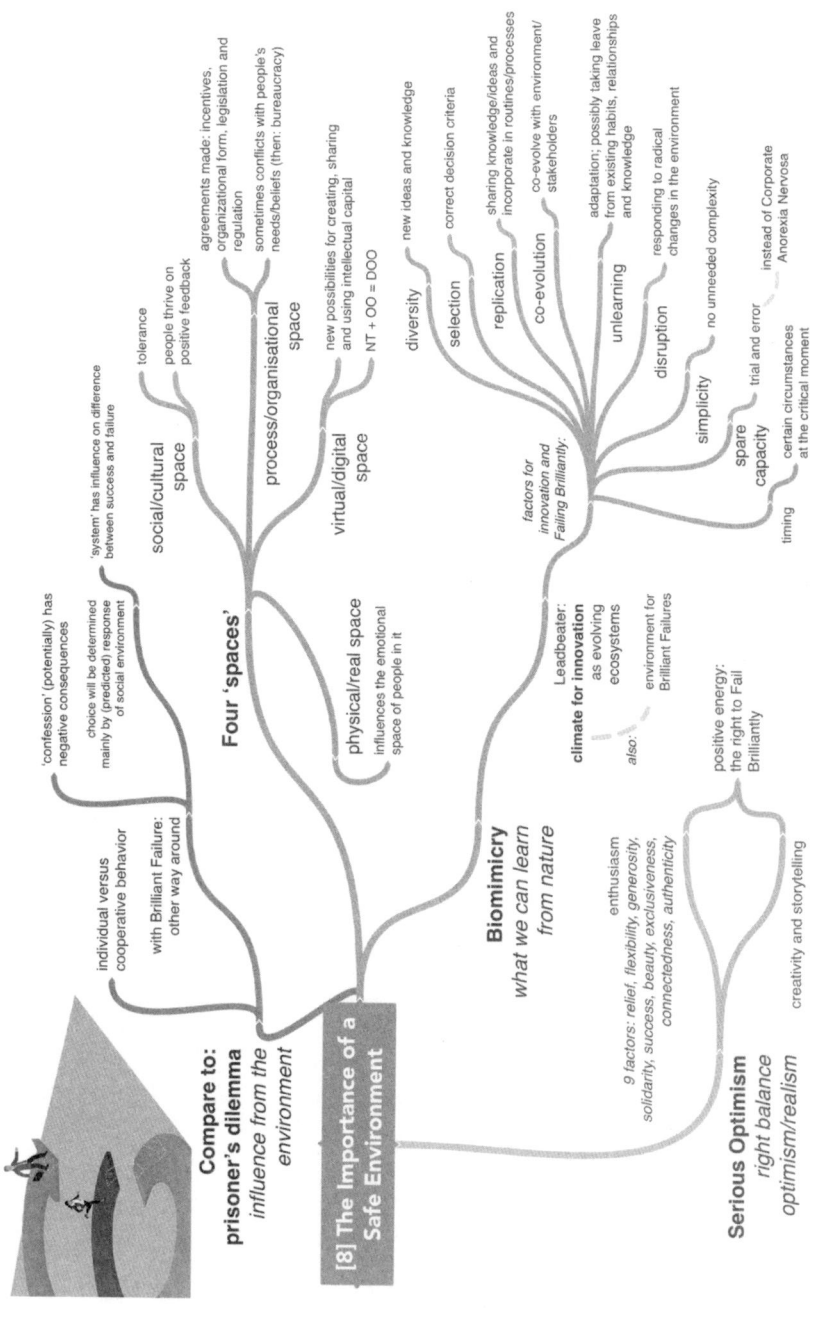

Compare to:
prisoner's dilemma
influence from the
environment

individual versus
cooperative behavior

with Brilliant Failure:
other way around

'confession' (potentially) has
negative consequences

choice will be determined
mainly by (predicted) response
of social environment

'system' has influence on difference
between success and failure

Four 'spaces'

social/cultural
space

tolerance

people thrive on
positive feedback

process/organisational
space

agreements made: incentives,
organizational form, legislation and
regulation

sometimes conflicts with people's
needs/beliefs (then: bureaucracy)

virtual/digital
space

new possibilities for creating, sharing
and using intellectual capital

NT + OO = DOO

diversity

new ideas and knowledge

selection

correct decision criteria

replication

sharing knowledge/ideas and
incorporate in routines/processes

co-evolution

co-evolve with environment/
stakeholders

unlearning

adaptation; possibly taking leave
from existing habits, relationships
and knowledge

disruption

responding to radical
changes in the environment

simplicity

no unneeded complexity

spare
capacity

trial and error

instead of Corporate
Anorexia Nervosa

timing

certain circumstances
at the critical moment

factors for
innovation and
Failing Brilliantly:

physical/real space
influences the emotional
space of people in it

Biomimicry
what we can learn
from nature

Leadbeater:
climate for innovation
as evolving
ecosystems

also:
environment for
Brilliant Failures

[8] The Importance of a
Safe Environment

positive energy:
the right to Fail
Brilliantly

enthusiasm

9 factors: relief, flexibility, generosity,
solidarity, success, beauty, exclusiveness,
connectedness, authenticity

creativity and storytelling

Serious Optimism
right balance
optimism/realism

9. THE INFLUENCE OF CULTURE ON FAILING BRILLIANTLY

On Culture

The word "culture" comes from the Latin verb *colere*, which includes such concepts as "cultivate," "cherish," and "fertility rites." Broadly speaking, it refers to anything produced by society, both material and immaterial. This description places culture in opposition to nature. The word is currently often used in a slightly different sense, to refer to a people's vision and way of life; their way of seeing, being and doing.

The Netherlands is a stereotypically tolerant country; the death penalty, for instance, is forbidden by the Dutch Constitution. Brilliantly Failed enterprises, however, tend to receive less mercy. Going bankrupt is much more frowned upon in the Netherlands than in the U.S., for example. An entrepreneur who has gone bankrupt before may struggle to get funding in the Netherlands, whereas in the U.S. they would be considered a rookie if they *hadn't* gone bankrupt before. Go ahead and get a few more years of experience before you come back asking for an investment!

At the tip of the iceberg, countries are characterized by such features as local currency, language, geography, climate, the dominant type of economic sectors, e.g. service sector, culture sector, manufacturing sector, and wealth. More fundamental characteristics are shaped by the often implicit norms, values, and beliefs held by the people of a country. In intercultural management issues, this is often the point where the Hofstede model comes in. Organizational psychology guru Geert Hofstede identifies six so-called cultural dimensions, which together form these more fundamental characteristics:

1. Power distance. This refers to the degree of inequality that exists between, and is accepted by, more powerful and less powerful people. A high score on this dimension indicates a large power distance, which means the society or culture in question has a high level of inequality. This implies the existence of rigid hierarchies—as is the case in most Asian countries, for example. A low score indicates a small power distance. These kinds of societies have a higher level of equality, as is the case in many Western European countries.

2. Individualism vs. collectivism. Individualism refers to the strength of the ties among individuals within a certain community. A high score on this dimension indicates loose ties. Individuals in these kinds of societies highly value their time and freedom. Respect for privacy and rewards for hard work are two other characteristics of societies with a high score. A low score indicates that a society is more collectivist, characterized by strong group cohesion, loyalty, and respect for members of one's in-group. The emphasis is on continuously developing skills that turn individuals into masters or experts. Other important characteristics of more collectivist societies are working for intrinsic rewards and valuing harmony over honesty.

3. Masculinity vs. femininity. Masculinity refers to the extent to which a society lives by its values in the form of traditional male and female roles. Masculine cultures emphasize achievement, heroism, and material rewards for success, whereas feminine cultures emphasize cooperation, modesty, tenderness, and quality of life. A low score on this dimension indicates a relatively small difference between men and women in the society in question. Women can also enter stereotypically male professions, cooperation is highly valued, and men are also allowed to be sensitive and caring.

4. Uncertainty avoidance. Uncertainty refers to the degree of anxiety experienced by members of a society when they encounter unfamiliar and ambiguous situations. A high score on this dimension indicates that uncertainties are avoided through control (rules and order). People in these kinds of societies seek a collective truth, expecting it to provide a certain degree of certainty. A low score indicates that new events and initiatives are welcomed; people in these kinds of societies are informal with each other and are open to change and taking risks.

5. Long-term orientation vs. short-term orientation. This dimension refers to societal values based on traditions and time-honored values, which are relevant in both the short term and the long term. A high score on this dimension indicates the following characteristics: Family is the cornerstone of society, education is highly valued, and older people and men have more authority than young people and women. This is mainly seen in Asian countries. A low score indicates a high degree of creativity and individualism. People treat each other as equals and help each other implement very innovative plans and ideas.

6. Indulgence vs. restraint. This dimension refers to cultures in which people are free to gratify their natural desires to enjoy life. The opposite is an environment with strict norms in place, restricting people's freedom to live life on their own terms.

The way a society deals with failure and Brilliant Failures can often be deduced from a combination of the above dimensions, which sometimes produces surprising results.

Brilliant Failures in the Netherlands Compared to Other Countries

The culture of failure in the Netherlands

Dutch culture is characterized by a high degree of individualism, long-term thinking, and respecting/valuing natural freedoms. It's hierarchically oriented to a very limited extent and strongly feminine. On the one hand, equality plays a major role; on the other hand, people are very focused on themselves and their immediate surroundings.

What does this mean when it comes to the way Brilliant Failures are dealt with? The Dutch generally aren't big on standing out from the crowd, so they don't necessarily value people taking risks to achieve some major goal. In the event of failure, sympathy isn't guaranteed. The Dutch aren't always open to sharing things, such as learning experiences, either. At the same time, they're not afraid of others—their superiors included—when something didn't work out and are relatively able to look beyond the here and now. All in all, this is an environment in which failure isn't disastrous, but people shouldn't expect appreciation for sticking their necks out either.

In addition, everyone in the Netherlands likes to have a say and to take part in the discussion. The advantage of this consensus-based approach is that decisions are often widely supported, but it also has disadvantages. It often takes a long time for something to be decided and it's often difficult to go back on a decision once it's been made, even if it later turns out that things could or should have been done differently. This may result in the archetype of "The Junk" (not being able to stop in time) rearing its head.

Geert Hofstede's research shows that only about 10 percent of the world population lives in countries that can be considered egalitarian: the U.S., the U.K., Germany, Switzerland, Austria, the Netherlands, and the Scandinavian countries. All other countries are more hierarchically oriented. It's interesting, then, to compare the culture of failure in the Netherlands to the culture of failure in several other countries around the world. We'll look at the U.S., Norway, Indonesia, South Korea, and Africa, based on interviews with and contributions by people with a connection to the countries in question.

The culture of failure in the U,S.
Contribution by Elizabeth Kleinveld, start-up matchmaker and angel investor

When considering the question of why start-ups fail and how these failures are perceived differently in the U.S. versus Europe, it's important to be aware of the influence of the adventurous spirit of the people who migrated to the New World. These people were on their own and had to rely on themselves to survive and succeed. The U.S. has a "sink or swim" mentality. If you can't swim, no one will come to save you and you will drown. In Europe, the dream Jeremy Rifkin reminds us of in his book *The European Dream* encourages us to ensure that we can work together as a community, taking care of people when they can't take care of themselves.

These considerations are relevant to understanding why start-ups and their investors in the U.S. are willing to take more risks. They realize that it's on themselves to make sure they succeed. Many founders of Silicon Valley start-ups know that not having failed several times may work to your disadvantage, as learning from failure helps you find the right approach. In his book *The Startup Way* (2017), Eric Ries states that the most successful entrepreneurs failed several times before they succeeded. Compared to the Netherlands, the U.S. is even more individualistic, much more masculine, and less long-term oriented. Going bankrupt in the Netherlands is more often seen as a problem because of people's relationships with others, such as their investors. You let them down! This factor is much less important in the U.S., where people are perhaps more opportunistic and more likely to try again. Another factor may be the importance of quarterly results in the U.S. (a result of shorter-term thinking). This quarter's bankruptcy won't show up in next quarter's results, so... Who cares?

One of the greatest start-up failures in history is described below. The knowledge gained from this failure, however, can be reused and might play a role in Amazon's attempt to permanently disrupt the retail sector.

Webvan

The intention

Webvan was launched in 1998, in the heyday of the dot-com era. The idea behind the company was that software could manage the inventory and delivery of all kinds of products, including groceries. The company was started by the Borders brothers, who managed to raise 150 million dollars in investments before going public.

The approach

The money was used to build the website and the logistics infrastructure, including delivery trucks and highly automated distribution centers. The company signed a one billion dollar contract to have 26 of these centers built.

The result

It turned out that Webvan insufficiently understood its customers. Most shoppers prefer to pick out their own fruits, vegetables and meats. They also like to use coupons, which Webvan initially didn't provide. In addition, people often make impulse purchases, whereas Webvan required its customers to order 24 hours in advance. Finally, people had to be home to accept delivery during a thirty-minute time slot that couldn't be changed. Only half of the people who tried out Webvan returned to place a second order.

The lessons learned

If the founders had done their homework and got to know their customers better, they would have been able to change their approach much faster. They also lacked knowledge of the grocery business, which has very low profit margins. The 26 distribution centers operated at only 35 percent of capacity and products were often damaged on the conveyor belts. The founders would have done better to use a growth model and take into account the shortcomings of previous distribution centers when designing new ones.

And there's more...
Perhaps the founders would have done even better to focus on the book industry. They had experience in this area, having founded the bookstore chain Borders which they eventually sold to Kmart. Webvan's vision was similar to Amazon's; they might even have become competitors. Amazon, which was founded in 1994 and is now a dominant player in the online retail business, is currently breaking into the online grocery business and will surely take advantage of the lessons learned from Webvan.

The boldness and drive with which Webvan was founded, and the investments made in the concept, could probably only have occurred in the U.S. at the time. Without revenue and healthy profit expectations, it never could've occurred in Europe. Europe simply has a different view of risk. This is where you can see the influence of the particularly masculine character of American culture, in which taking risks and having an all-or-nothing attitude are much more common than in the Netherlands; where more value is attached to taking care of each other. And failure means not having taken proper care of each other.

The lessons people in Europe can learn from the American vision of start-ups is that start-ups have to be careful not to use up their funds too quickly. If they do, they'll run the risk of failing to scale because their focus will shift too quickly to earning revenue and therefore to preventing minor or early mistakes, which are in fact indispensable for finding sustainable success.

The culture of failure in Norway
Contribution by Truls Berg, Internet entrepreneur

Norway was originally a farming community where everyone helped each other out when needed. This is still visible today, for example in the typically Norwegian concept of *dugnad*, which refers to a kind of community day when people fix things, paint, and tidy up together. Norway is an egalitarian society with a high degree of cooperation. In addition, Norway—with its mountain ranges and its four seasons—was no place for people who wanted to sit in the shade of a palm tree, waiting for the fruit to fall down. Instead, they rolled up their sleeves and took action. Historians also cite the lack of nobility in Norway as an explanation for the fact that managers in organizations aren't regarded with awe the way they are in many other countries. In practice, there's actually little difference between boss and employee in Norwegian organizations.

The traditional Norwegian culture is very inclusive: Everyone is treated with respect and pointing out other people's mistakes is considered impolite. Norwegian employers essentially have a long tradition of sweeping problems under the rug for the sake of the higher purpose of keeping up the mood at all costs.

The general view is that accepting mistakes is important for successful innovation, and that it's actually good to talk about failure in order to learn from it. This idea is still new in Norway and only implemented in organizations to a very limited extent. In innovative, fast-growing Norwegian companies, a shift can be seen toward goals related to quality of life and more holistic thinking, including paying attention to people, planet, and profit. But a generation ago, it was perfectly normal for employees to be promoted simply because they'd been with the company for a long time. In such a context, it's better not to pay too much attention to failures.

With the underlying idea that all roads lead to Rome, Norwegian managers often discuss issues broadly, as a result of which they need a lot of time to reach a decision. This inclusive approach is similar to the Dutch consensus-based approach. Some see it as a sign of weakness, but Norwegians see this differently because they value networking. Almost 98 percent of all companies in Norway are SMEs and SMEs need partnerships, even though these require time and effort and contribute to the increasing complexity of the business landscape. While an American leader may decide and act quickly, the pace in network-oriented cultures such as Norway and the Netherlands is generally much slower. These cultures could take to heart the lessons shared by Daniel Kahneman in his book *Thinking, Fast and Slow* (2011). Because so much time and effort goes into making a decision, it's often difficult to admit that it may not have been the best decision after all and failure will often go unstated or at least unstated for too long. In addition, it's often difficult to talk to each other about failures; the decision was a joint one, after all.

But change is happening. There are signs that Norway is now a little more open to both successes and failures and, yes, even to the view that both successes and failures are necessary in order to play a significant role amid the world leaders in innovation. "Innovation made in Norway" could create new forms of value creation in Norway, based on its cultural ideology in which everyone is equal and the feminine side can offer protection if things go really wrong. The fact that Norway has for several decades been called "Lotto-Landet," the Lottery Country, because of its natural riches (natural beauty, oil reserves, hydropower) also makes it slightly easier to fail here, of course. But this gives Norway the opportunity to experiment and learn from things that don't work. The term Brilliant Failures, or "Briljante Fiaskoene," will probably be increasingly heard in Norway!

Linie Aquavit

The intention

The concept of Linie Aquavit originated in Norway in the nineteenth century. Aquavit is a potato-based liquor, flavored with caraway seeds. Jørgen Lysholm owned an aquavit distillery in the Norwegian town of Trondheim. Lysholm's mother and uncle wanted to boost his business and started looking for new markets abroad.

The approach

They sent a batch of aquavit to Asia on a large sailing ship with the aim of putting it on the market there.

The result

It didn't work out; the product didn't sell. Five casks were shipped back to Trondheim. When they arrived there, Lysholm noticed that the spirit had a richer flavor. At the time, Norway was shipping dried cod around the world. Lysholm began to send casks of aquavit along as deck cargo, retrieving them after their long trip around the world to bottle the liquor. To this day, Linie Aquavit is produced this way. It's shipped across the equator in oak casks, to Australia and back again. The inside of the label of each bottle tells you when and on which ship the liquor in it made the trip.

The lessons learned

This is an example of serendipity, being open to an alternative form of success. By the way, attempts were made to mechanize the enrichment process by shaking the liquor in casks for weeks. According to experts, however, the result of this can't hold a candle to the classic method.

The culture of failure in Indonesia

Contribution by Rennie Roos and Thierry Sanders, social entre-preneurs (founders of BiD Network Foundation)

Compared to the Netherlands, Indonesia is much more hierar-chical, much less individualistic, considerably more masculine, and more focused on the immediate gratification of needs. Indonesians are a very social people who love to chat and do things together. The word *desama,* doing things together, is everywhere. In Indonesia, everyone is quiet and when the lea-der or manager says "Stop discussing and get to work," every-one gets to work.

In Indonesia, losing face is one of the worst things that can happen to a person. If a mistake has been made, they prefer not to acknowledge it and avoid talking about it as long as possible. But this results in an accumulation of new mistakes. And in this way, something might go wrong for months, but they don't dare tell their boss about it. They prefer to try to solve the pro-blem themselves, which has both economic and social conse-quences. After all, the sooner you realize you made a mistake, the better. It'll have less serious consequences that way.

The Dutch don't like to make mistakes either, but they are to some extent aware that mistakes provide opportunities for learning. This is much less the case in Indonesia, where people often strive for a false sense of security, for example by drawing up extensive contracts. This is especially seen in large compa-nies. All official documents end up in a huge folder, on which a lot of time is spent.

Another aspect of Indonesian culture is that there are a lot of entrepreneurs. Paradoxically, people often become entrepre-neurs to reduce risks, as there's no social safety net in Indone-sia. Many people—managers included—run a small business in addition to their work. This way, if one of their sources of income dries up, they'll always have another way to earn their living.

BiD Network

The intention
BiD Network was established with the goal of helping entrepreneurs with growth potential in emerging markets by giving them access to expertise and capital. Over a period of five years, BiD Network grew to be the largest online platform for entrepreneurs in emerging markets.

The approach
Aided by funding, BiD Network established its own web platform, BiDx. BiDx offers online portals to organizations involved in the development of SMEs, such as banks, accelerators, funds, accountants and consultants. These organizations can use BiDx to build their own communities for entrepreneurs, investors and coaches. The platform matches entrepreneurs with coaches for advice and coaching, and with investors for financing. In 2010, BiD Network won the prestigious G-20 SME Finance Challenge with BiDx.

The result
Initially, a few things went wrong. First of all, we put too much faith in technology. We thought there were enough checks and balances in the system to filter out the bad companies before a loan was approved. We also assumed that we would be informed in time if something went wrong. These two things combined caused a lot of trouble. A number of hired intermediaries turned out to be corrupt and circumventing the rules, which shouldn't have been possible. And our employees who found out about this didn't dare tell us about it for months. This cost a lot of money in irrecoverable loans. This is a negative consequence of the fear of talking about something at the bottom of the ladder, causing the problem to get bigger and bigger.

The culture of failure in South Korea
*Contribution by Boohwan Byun, South Korean expat in the
Netherlands and assistant professor at Sogang University, Seoul*

Shortly after the Second World War, Korea was one of the
poorest countries in the world. After the Korean War, South
Korea started developing rapidly. The country worked hard,
embraced the knowledge economy, shot up in the rankings,
and is now relatively high on the list when it comes to welfare and wellbeing. This progress is especially discernible in the
area of industrialization, as illustrated by the emergence of
large companies such as Samsung, LG, KIA, and Hyundai. The
development of the country is very much seen as a collective
achievement.

It's difficult to talk about failures in South Korea. This can
be immediately understood based on an analysis of the culture of the country. There's a great distance between the
different levels in South Korean organizations. This affects
the climate of failure in two ways. For example, subordinates
are afraid to ask questions and even more afraid to tell their
superiors that something went wrong. People in senior positions feel responsible and feel like admitting to failure causes
them to lose face. People are also very risk averse. This has
many consequences. For example, there's a lack of creativity and entrepreneurship. South Korea has a limited social
safety net, as a result of which many young people prefer to
take government jobs. There's also a lot of bureaucracy. If
you stick to the rules, not much can go wrong. South Korea
has many family businesses and, because of the hierarchy,
all major decisions are made directly by the owner/boss. In
companies whose owners or bosses are willing to take risks,
experimentation and failure are not taboo subjects. Large
companies often have more room for experimentation and
failure. A good example of this is the Samsung Galaxy Note 7

fiasco. This device turned out to have a defect, causing it to catch fire spontaneously. The exact cause was never determined, which only goes to show how complex these kinds of products are. This Brilliant Failure is a classic example of the Einstein Point archetype (too complex), although it also contains a number of other ingredients to do with the commercial pressure to bring the product to market quickly and the initial denial of the problem. The interesting thing about this situation is that Samsung didn't really make a big deal out of it, despite the enormous amount of financial and temporary reputational damage caused by the recall of the device. Life goes on, the company's financial position is fine—partly because of its semiconductor business—and no one was fired.

It's also interesting that companies such as Apple and Samsung aren't poster children for democratic, flat organizations. Steve Jobs didn't exactly believe in servant leadership either, which are often described in studies of innovation.

At a more individual level, the subject of failure is much more sensitive. Precisely because of the combination of hierarchy, collectivism, long-term thinking and risk aversion, the social norm is that losing face is relatively unacceptable in organizations, families, or society as a whole. Few cases of burnout are reported in South Korea, as burnout is seen as a personal failure. But—and partly because of this—the suicide rate in South Korea is very high, the highest among OECD countries. In particular, relatively older women often commit suicide in South Korea. It's interesting and encouraging to see that the suicide rate among young people is lower, although still almost twice as high as in the Netherlands.

There are, of course, various reasons why someone might consider something as drastic as suicide. At a macro level at least, South Korea is faring reasonably well economically speaking; there hasn't been a severe financial or economic crisis. The economic growth rate was 2.9% even in the crisis year of 2013. In this respect, then, South Korea certainly doesn't do poorly compared to other countries. The causes of the country's high suicide rate are more fundamental, and the intolerance of failure clearly plays a role in this. In the last few years, several high government officials in South Korea have ended their own lives after allegations of mismanagement.

In conclusion, it can be stated that failure is not accepted in South Korea and people are very aware of this fact. A campaign to emphasize the importance and value of experimentation and learning from unexpected experiences, failures included, could have a positive social impact.

The culture of failure in Africa
Contribution by Emiel Hanekamp, sustainability consultant specialized in Africa

Of course, it's difficult to conduct a thorough analysis of African culture in just a few words, if only because the major differences that exist between the various African countries also affect the perception of risk and failure in these different countries. But compared to the Netherlands, there are several characteristic differences. The power distance and degree of masculinity are considerably greater in Africa, while people are much less individualistic and much less long-term oriented.

One of the reasons why dealing with and learning from failures in most African countries is difficult is that giving negative feedback, especially in public, is simply not done. Learning from failures involving both African and Western parties is complicated by virtually all cultural characteristics.

A good, generally accepted example of this is the entirely different way Europeans and Africans conceive of time. Europeans see time as a linear phenomenon. Projects are planned as a series of sequential steps. The focus is on the deadline and sticking to the schedule. The emphasis is on punctuality and good organization over flexibility. This also has to do with their long-term orientation. Africans see time as a more flexible phenomenon and are not terribly interested in the distant future. Project steps aren't carved in stone time-wise. Tasks are performed when convenient, multitasking occurs, and interruptions are accepted. The focus is on adaptability and flexibility over organization. While this does involve a learning component, knowledge isn't consciously developed and definitely not sustainably stored and/or shared.

Both of these completely different approaches are rooted in the extent to which people have to deal with daily uncertainties, such as uncertainty about the question of whether they will arrive at their destination because of unexpected heavy rain and flooded streets and roads. Or uncertainty about the question of whether there will be electricity—and therefore Internet, cell phone service, printing facilities, etc. Or uncertainty about the question of whether it's even a workday; there are several countries where the decision that the next day is a holiday is made only a day in advance.

A potentially positive factor in accepting and learning from failures could be the fact that people in Africa—compared to, for example, people in the Netherlands—are more collectively oriented. "Collective" here refers primarily to local communities. Perhaps this is also the key to more acceptance of and learning from Brilliant Failures. In the local collective, people can tell their stories and will be more willing to accept and apply the knowledge gained.

The following example shows a failure caused by a number of cultural factors, both in the world of professional soccer and between two different countries.

Chinese takeover of ADO Den Haag
Contribution by Jasmine Chang

The period from early 2014 to January 2017 was certainly not an easy one for Mr. Wang, a wealthy businessman from Beijing. International mergers and acquisitions are rarely easy, but the takeover of the 111-year-old Dutch soccer club ADO Den Haag proved even more difficult than expected. The way this deal was portrayed in the Dutch press ranged from "life-saving action" to "complete failure."

The intention
Wang's marketing company, United Vansen International Sports, wanted to take over ADO Den Haag (which hasn't won the national championship since the Second World War and hasn't won the Dutch Cup since 1975) and make it a top-tier club. The goal: Going European. Wang also announced that he would send Dutch coaches to China to help develop young soccer talent. This strategy was in line with the Chinese government's foreign investment policy at the time; Wang Hui was definitely not the first Chinese businessman to invest in a European soccer club.

The approach
The 8.9 million dollar takeover took place in late 2014. The club met its new owner in January 2015. Although Wang Hui promised to invest 4.1 million dollars in the club, he missed payments in September and November 2015. Wang indicated

that he wouldn't pay until he was given clarification on the club's expenses. In September 2015, China's former national coach Gao Hongbo arrived in the Netherlands on a business visa with the intention of becoming assistant coach. No one in the Netherlands knew about this. ADO Den Haag's coach at the time, Henk Fraser, was asked if he was being replaced. He replied, "To be honest, I've only talked to him a few times. In any case, he's not part of my training staff."

The result
In 2015 ADO Den Haag's general director resigned, citing differences in strategic vision. Because of the deferred payments, the club faced a liquidity crisis in January 2016 and was placed under the supervision of the Royal Dutch Football Association (KNVB), the governing body of soccer in the Netherlands. Wang insisted on more transparency, but ADO Den Haag demanded payment instead. Wang's suggestion to have a Chinese manager investigate the matter was rejected. A meeting of shareholders was held, but Wang didn't show up. His son came to a second meeting. ADO Den Haag's supporters accused Wang of untrustworthy behavior and deplored his absenteeism. The club eventually took Wang to court and won in November 2016. The promised payment was made at the end of January 2017, but ADO Den Haag is still under the supervision of the KNVB.

The lessons learned
It's interesting to consider this situation from the other side as well. Wang repeatedly indicated that he wanted to know what ADO Den Haag had done with his money: "You've apparently taken an advance on my investment, but what have you spent it on?" What Wang didn't realize is that ownership didn't mean he was in charge; officially, the daily management of a Dutch soccer club is with its management team.

The Chinese businessman's straightforward logic said "No plan, no money," but the agreement said something else: "Pay up whether or not there's a solution to our conflict."

This process was frustrated by the physical and cultural distance. Trusted Chinese intermediaries are often used in Chinese-European enterprises. When this failed, Wang's trust was gone. Chinese parent companies often try to force the more collectivist Chinese culture onto generally more individualistically oriented Western companies. And it's always easier to attribute failure to "cultural differences" than to perhaps avoidable mistakes, right?

The project was also complicated by practical matters. Famous former soccer player Gao Hongbo's transfer couldn't go through because of Dutch immigration laws and transfer regulations for soccer players and coaches to Europe.

And there's more...
It has been suggested that the billions of investments in almost twenty soccer clubs were largely fueled by Chinese President Xi Jinping's love of soccer. In 2017, however, the Chinese government adopted a stricter foreign investment policy, explicitly prohibiting investments in soccer clubs. This raises the question of what future there is for the associations involved. How many of them will experience a Brilliant Failure?

Failure in the Context of Government
The government is a special world to work for or with. The government is omnipresent and plays various roles in our society. Sometimes it's a regulator, sometimes it's a partner, sometimes it's a service provider, and so on. The government is a many-headed monster encompassing various environments and cultures. For example, there's a big difference between politics and the civil service. Various conversations have made clear to me

how the government deals with risks and failures. The world of politics is not very forgiving: The opposition is always at the ready to pounce on any misstep, without distinguishing much between Brilliant Failures and more culpable mistakes. On top of that, there's the public exposure. The role of the media is to identify and verify issues and put them on the agenda. But focusing on things that don't go well leads to a distorted view of reality and high risk aversion. The influence of the media and public opinion regularly influences the political agenda. This isn't a problem in and of itself—it ensures that issues that are considered relevant are addressed—but it shouldn't result in the postponement of complex and thorny issues to escape immediate judgment. We must be careful not to replace democracy with adhocracy. Risky issues and projects are sometimes avoided because the amount of recognition for success (the upside) is much smaller than the amount of criticism in case of failure (the downside). The effects of this can also be seen in the civil service, which also carefully considers the possible consequences of a new approach for the position of the alderperson, undersecretary, or minister responsible. It's no secret that members of the government often have to step down because of issues they weren't even personally involved in—and regardless of whether they gave it their all and got up every morning to deal as well as possible with the large-scale, complex kinds of issues the government has to deal with. The proverbial banana peel can take various forms, from personal controversies such as sex scandals or the use of a private server for work-related emails, to secret recordings. It's not about whether the consequences are fair, but about the fact that members of the government really have to walk on eggshells sometimes, regardless of their often good intentions. We don't need to feel sorry for anyone in particular, but when people start avoiding certain risks in their work out of fear, or feeling like they have to conceal their failures, the question is justified whether this serves the public interest.

Contribution by Maarten Camps, Secretary-General at the Netherlands Ministry of Economic Affairs and Climate Policy

Complex issues should be approached with boldness more often. Simply getting started with promising proposals allows the government to gain experience, based on which targeted adjustments can be made. This way, social issues at both the national and the European level can be addressed and stalemates can be resolved.

Major issues that will require attention in coming years include the transition to a circular economy, food supply, secure digitization, the energy transition, the labor market, and healthcare. Boldly approaching complex issues implies that citizens and companies are involved, starting with targeted policy and adjusting it when necessary. In this process, it's important to dare to accept the uncertainties associated with innovation and change (Camps, 2016). Uncertainty too often causes a standstill, leaving opportunities unused. Much attention is paid to the risks and uncertainties of policy.

The need for a bold approach partly follows from the increasingly dynamic context in which policy is made. Dynamism implies the need to adapt legislation more frequently, but these kinds of adaptations take relatively much time. There's social dynamism as well. Nowadays, citizens and companies have more skills and tools at their disposal to gather and process information, as well as more opportunities to express their opinions, especially through digital communication. This both complicates and enriches policy practice: Citizens more easily unite to thwart new developments, but they also roll up their sleeves to protect public interests on their own initiative more often.

In a dynamic and interwoven world, the traditional way of developing policy is no longer always appropriate. This raises the question of whether there are more effective ways to solve complex problems. The answer to this question consists of three steps: involving citizens and companies to arrive at common goals, starting with concrete and targeted instruments, and adjusting policy based on factual information. This requires boldness. This boldness is still too often lacking, causing arguments to be repeated, investigations to be launched, and actual steps to be postponed. This is because we focus on minimizing risks, the precautionary principle. By getting started with promising proposals, we can create room for the innovation principle.

"Getting started" may also mean setting up an experiment and learning from it (Van Geest, 2016). It may be wise to initially design a small-scale, incremental, or simulation experiment. Sometimes, however, the intended learning effect requires a larger scale, larger steps, or a start in the "real" world, nationally or together with other countries. Whichever experimental design is chosen, the essence is always the same: The government makes an intervention, learns from information about its effects, and adjusts the intervention if necessary.

Experimentation requires good preparation, together with the parties involved. Experiments yield valuable information, enabling the government to better serve its citizens and companies and achieve social goals.

Experiments enable learning, help generate new ideas, and bring the desired effects closer. That's what it's all about in the end. Because in order to realize social goals, we must dare to explore new paths.

The Electronic Health Record (EHR) project

Contribution by Marcelis Boereboom, Director-General at the Netherlands Ministry of Education, Culture and Science

On March 1, 2008, I became director-general for the first time: Director-General Long-Term Care at the Netherlands Ministry of Health, Welfare and Sport. In addition to being responsible for long-term care, I was responsible for introducing a national Electronic Health Record (EHR) system in the Netherlands.

I was very personally motivated. As a person suffering from multiple chronic conditions, with various healthcare providers, various diets, and nine different medications, I knew how important having an EHR could be. Much more importantly, though, the political and social conditions at the time seemed favorable. The subject of developing a national EHR system had already been broached in the early 2000's, and a recent motion introduced in the House of Representatives urged the cabinet to move quickly now.

The decisions we made seemed brilliant to me. Rather than there being one large database, each healthcare provider retained its own record, which could be accessed by other patient-approved healthcare providers via a national switch point. In case of emergency, any healthcare provider could get access, but they'd have to justify this. Also, each access was logged, and Dutch citizens could indicate whether they wanted to participate through informed consent. The House of Representatives seemed satisfied and the underlying bill was passed by a large majority. With such broad support, combined with strong advocacy from one of the ministers, its chances of clearing the Senate seemed good. This turned out to be an illusion.

First of all, some members of the Senate were not convinced that the issue of privacy had been sufficiently addressed. They also, and especially, questioned the usefulness and necessity of a national EHR system. Wasn't this a far too complex solution to a relatively simple problem? A major national newspaper ran various highly critical articles on the subject. The Dutch Data Protection Authority was also very critical, as was the Rathenau Institute (a member of the European Parliamentary Technology Assessment) consulted by the Senate.

Perhaps even more important was the resistance from the healthcare industry itself, in which family doctors played a significant role. At the time, there were two other important issues at play that interfered with the EHR project. First of all, a new Healthcare Insurance Act had just been passed, which met with resistance in some parts of the industry. There were concerns that health insurance companies would become too influential and would implement selective contracting if they knew the cost burden caused by their clients. Most important, though, was the fear that health insurance companies would gain access to the EHR system.

Another issue was the public debate on unnecessary deaths in healthcare and the public debate on inter-physician variation. Wouldn't the EHR system, anonymized, be particularly suitable for assessing the quality of healthcare? Couldn't it be used for peer review to improve the quality of care? Healthcare providers, however, were very concerned about the possibility of health insurance companies using these data to implement selective contracting.

Because all of these developments, the Senate became increasingly doubtful. Eventually, the proposed bill was unanimously rejected.

In an interview I did when I left the Ministry of Health, Welfare and Sport, I called the failure of the EHR project my greatest professional disappointment. It remains so to this day. But it's also my most important learning experience, together with the bankruptcy of home care organization Meavita.

The first learning experience was that issues should always be considered in context. The EHR project came too soon after the new Healthcare Insurance Act and interfered with public debates on selective contracting and patient safety. Secondly, we knew much less about the Internet then than we do now. The timing was simply off. Thirdly, it once again became clear that there's a major difference between rationality and emotionality, both of which are equally relevant and valuable. Fourthly, personal investment is good, but it also makes us run the risk of tunnel vision—especially if the cabinet minister, director-general and project leader involved are all equally motivated. Finally, the healthcare industry should've been involved much more closely in retrospect. And for us, by definition, the parliament enjoys great respect and is always right.

Erik Gerritsen is Secretary-General at the Netherlands Ministry of Health, Welfare and Sport and very actively helping to improve the climate for innovation in the healthcare industry. We asked him what characterizes the relationship between the healthcare industry and failures. His answer: "The healthcare industry engages in autopoiesis thinking. This is a term from biology and literally means self-production. In biology, given the right context and the presence of the right components, a system can arise by itself and sustain itself. Now, every system is inherently conservative. At a certain point it no longer matches the challenges of its environment and transformation of the 'system world' becomes necessary. The Dutch healthcare system is especially conservative. There are two causes for this. Firstly, healthcare in the Netherlands is relatively good, so why change it?

It's better to get sick in the Netherlands than in most other countries. Secondly, we've created these mental prisons where 'we want to but we can't': I want to but it's not allowed, it won't get funded, privacy won't allow it... The question is whether this isn't partly self-inflicted pain.

"The healthcare industry is under a microscope, even more so than other industries. This makes sense: Patients or clients who need care are entirely dependent on others. A failure on the part of these others could have serious or even fatal consequences. This is why trust is a key concept in the healthcare industry. It's also important that health professionals can safely learn and improve. This sometimes raises questions, as incidents in the healthcare industry are often magnified and professionals may also face disciplinary or legal action—which is, of course, a daunting thought. For example, there are various ongoing experiments with medical data recorders. These 'operating room black boxes' record images and sounds for learning purposes. But unlike in the aviation industry, the recorded data can be used by the Public Prosecution Service or the Health Care Inspectorate. The Inspectorate has already indicated that it will exercise maximum restraint in requesting these data, as it also prioritizes the importance of learning and improving. But the legal authority still exists; the Inspectorate can't change anything about that. This, then, requires mutual trust—not just the patient's and the Inspectorate's trust in the health professional, but also the health professional's trust in the Inspectorate actually creating room for them to learn and improve.

"Of course things go wrong sometimes, even in youth protection. It remains 'human work,' involving constant assessment, and mistakes can occur in this process. That's why there are still children who unnecessarily suffer abuse. But the alternative is doing nothing—which would result in all the children involved continuing to suffer abuse. Doctors, too, could state that if they didn't treat anyone, they wouldn't make any mistakes. But imagine being the parent of a child who was hurt because of a surgeon's error. Because it's about people, the risk aversion is even more difficult to overcome."

Erik Gerritsen's Brilliant Failure

The intention
Erik had a formative experience when he was a municipal clerk in 2006, dealing with cases involving multi-problem families causing nuisance in Amsterdam. Erik decided on his tried-and-true approach: Get the whole system in the room and let all parties involved solve the problem together. Rather than getting stuck in the system world, tell the professionals, "Just solve it. If you run into trouble, go to your bosses." The intention was to scale up this successful approach.

The approach
Everything in the first projects had gone well: concrete, practice-related, everyone involved. This approach was scaled up to two hundred families, after which the rest of the Amsterdam region would follow. In accordance with the logic of "don't reinvent the wheel," the following method was used to roll out the approach: Write it down, distribute it, spend a few days training people, and Bob's your uncle.

The result
But the rollout of the approach went awry. The people who had come up with and developed the approach were not the people it was being rolled out to; they didn't have the same experience and knowledge. This resulted in a difficult, lengthy, and uphill rollout process, without the "rollout recipients" mastering the approach.

The lessons learned
Don't roll out; roll up. Everyone has to go through their own learning process, reinvent the wheel for themselves, and master the practice that way. Good practices developed

elsewhere can at best serve as sources of inspiration and accelerate learning processes, but an approach that's simply rolled out will be dead on arrival.

A "rollup" involving one organization with one boss turned out to be possible. But from one organization to another is an entirely different story. To sum up the lessons learned:

- The greatest success can become the greatest failure.
- Beware of a perception of arrogance.
- Organizing a conference to toot your own horn is the best way to kill a good practice.

Applying Chapter 9

1. Assess how your environment/organization scores on the Hofstede dimensions and try to determine the characteristics of this cultural profile with regard to failure and dealing with failure. What are the supporting characteristics and where are the obstacles? What is needed to help change the culture in favor of experimentation and learning?
2. In which areas is the government allowed to fail, in your opinion? In which areas is it not allowed to fail?

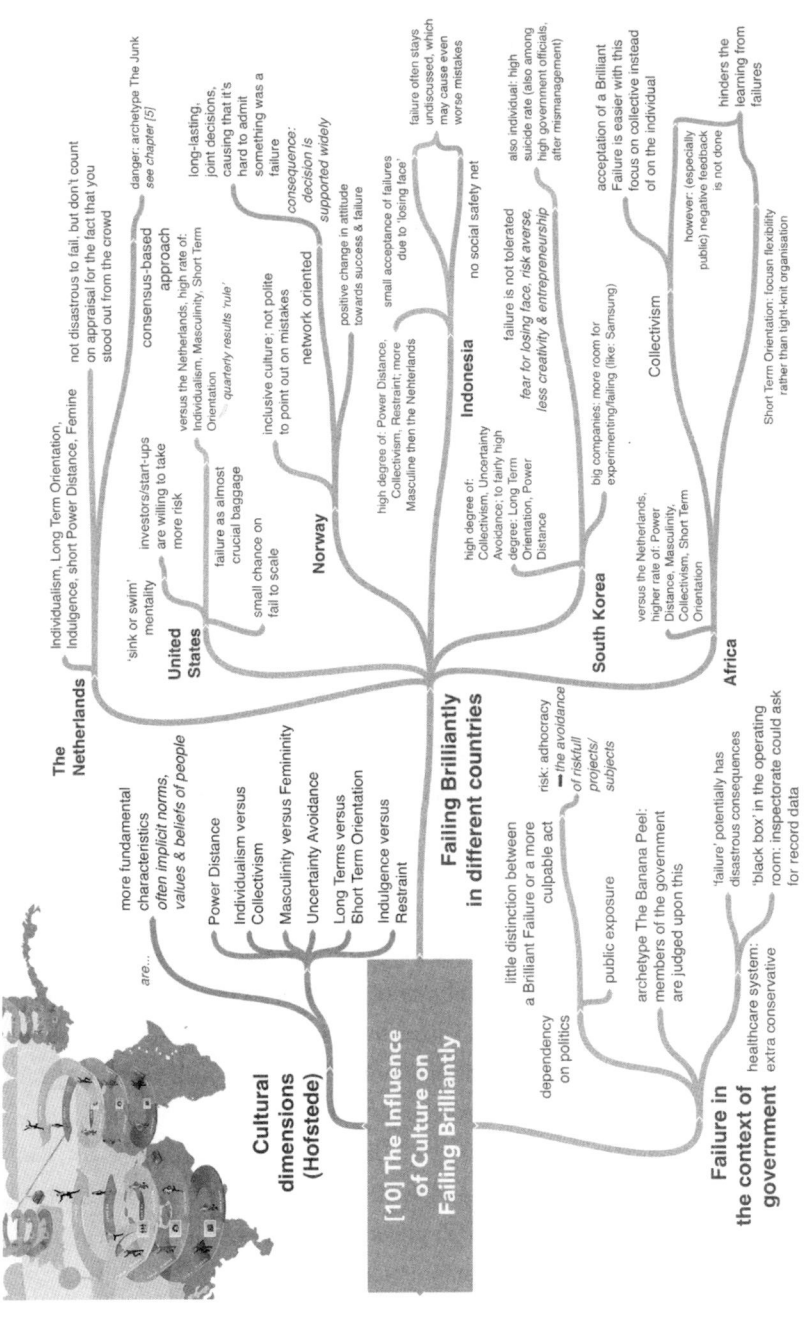

[10] The Influence of Culture on Failing Brilliantly

Cultural dimensions (Hofstede)

are...
- more fundamental characteristics *often implicit norms, values & beliefs of people*
- Power Distance
- Individualism versus Collectivism
- Masculinity versus Femininity
- Uncertainty Avoidance
- Long Terms versus Short Term Orientation
- Indulgence versus Restraint

Failing Brilliantly in different countries

- little distinction between a Brilliant Failure or a more culpable act
- public exposure
- dependency on politics
- risk: adhocracy — *the avoidance of riskfull projects/ subjects*

Failure in the context of government

- archetype The Banana Peel: members of the government are judged upon this
- 'failure' potentially has disastrous consequences
- 'black box' in the operating room: inspectorate could ask for record data
- healthcare system: extra conservative

The Netherlands

- Individualism, Long Term Orientation, Indulgence, short Power Distance, Femine
- not disastrous to fail, but don't count on appraisal for the fact that you stood out from the crowd
- consensus-based approach
  - danger: archetype The Junk *see chapter [5]*
  - versus the Netherlands: high rate of: Individualism, Masculinity, Short Term Orientation
  - long-lasting, joint decisions, causing that it's hard to admit something was a failure
    - *quarterly results 'rule'*
    - *consequence: decision is supported widely*
- inclusive culture: not polite to point out on mistakes
- network oriented
- positive change in attitude towards success & failure

United States

- 'sink or swim' mentality
- investors/start-ups are willing to take more risk
- failure as almost crucial baggage
- small chance on fail to scale

Norway

- small acceptance of failures due to 'losing face'
- no social safety net

Indonesia

- high degree of: Power Distance, Collectivism, Restraint; more Masculine then the Netherlands
- failure is not tolerated *fear for losing face, risk averse, less creativity & entrepreneurship*
- also individual: high suicide rate (also among high government officials, after mismanagement)

South Korea

- high degree of: Collectivism, Uncertainty Avoidance; to fairly high degree: Long Term Orientation, Power Distance
- big companies: more room for experimenting/failing (like: Samsung)

Collectivism

- acceptance of a Brilliant Failure is easier with this focus on collective instead of on the individual
- however: (especially public) negative feedback is not done
- hinders the learning from failures

Africa

- versus the Netherlands, higher rate of: Power Distance, Masculinity, Collectivism, Short Term Orientation
- Short Term Orientation: focuss flexibility rather than tight-knit organisation
- failure often stays undiscussed, which may cause even worse mistakes

203

10. THE INSTITUTE OF BRILLIANT FAILURES (IoBF)

The IoBF Knowledge Environment: BriFa Learning Environment

The IoBF has started developing an interactive knowledge environment, the BriFa learning environment, which makes contributing knowledge about your ongoing project or activity attractive and easy. The IoBF website is the first visible element of this public knowledge environment. It provides access to various aspects of the kind of knowledge the Institute gathers and shares, including a number of detailed case studies.

The previous chapters have introduced the main ideas and several concepts, such as the archetypes and the BriFa learning spiral. The archetypes play an important role in sharing failures because of their narrative form that appeals to the imagination. They contain part of the story, sometimes serving as the protagonist (the General Without an Army, the Acapulco Cliff Diver, the Junk) but more often serving as the antagonist (the Elephant, the Wrong Wallet, the Bridge of Choluteca, the Canyon, the Einstein Point, the Right Hemisphere, the Bear's Skin, the Empty Seat at the Table, the Banana Peel, the Black Swan, the Farmer's Daughter, the Light Bulb, the Winner Takes it All).

The BriFa learning spiral can help you determine at which stage of the learning process you currently are: "before," "during," or "after."

The common language that arises through the use of the archetypes and the evolutionary spiral has proven invaluable in sharing knowledge.

The BriFa learning environment, then, is partly a knowledge system, containing knowledge, and partly a knowledge information system, containing information that indicates which knowledge is available and where it can be found, including the knowledge carriers: people.

IoBF Intervention: *Journal of Brilliant Failures*

Virtually all scholarly or semi-scholarly journals emphasize the reporting of positive research findings. Project reports also tend to focus primarily on successful results and their substantiation. It's very rare to find a description of the struggles involved, the wrong turns taken, internal problems and unintended outcomes. It could be stated that people are more interested in results than in knowledge itself.

What to think of the story of the researcher whose article was published, after which she discovered that one of the assumptions was wrong? She found that the conclusions in her article were incorrect as a result and wrote a second article to correct the first one. The publisher who'd published the first article refused to publish the second one!

Leading journals still don't publish many negative research findings. According to Joeri Tijdink, a psychiatrist and researcher at VU University Amsterdam, many scholars and publishers suffer from "*Publiphilia Impact-factorius*," an obsession with achieving high-impact publications. The fear of getting fewer citations for papers reporting on null-result research continues to make it difficult to share lessons learned from negative findings. This has negative consequences for individual researchers, but also for the research field as a whole, because knowledge and resources are unnecessarily wasted. Perhaps hypotheses and methodologies should be guiding principles for publication. If the hypothesis and the methodology are well founded and the research is solid, i.e. conducted according to established academic standards, the result is relevant regardless of the outcome.

On a brighter note, various initiatives to turn the tide are emerging. For example, more and more journals and institutes require scholars to publish online their raw data, materials, and codes and procedures used, inspired by the #OPENSCIENCE movement. Journals such as the Journal of Negative Results in BioMedicine and the Journal of Negative Results in Ecology and Evolutionary Biology claim to pay an increasing amsount of attention to negative research findings.

The Institute of Brilliant Failures has taken the initiative to publish the *Journal of Brilliant Failures*, the first edition of which was published in December 2017. This healthcare-themed edition includes the ten cases that were nominated for the Brilliant Failure Award Health 2017.

Figure 21. The Dutch Journal of Brilliant Failures – *Healthcare Edition,*
No. 1, December 2017, and No. 2, December 2018

IoBF Intervention: Brilliant Failure Award

A fun way to create more awareness and understanding of entrepreneurship and dealing with risks, experimentation, and learning is organizing a
competition for the Brilliant Failure Award. During this process, the parties involved discuss the importance of accepting certain risks, accepting
things that go differently than hoped or expected, and the importance of
learning from all experiences. To align this message with the environment
in question, encourage recognizability and find concrete opportunities
for learning from failed activities, the approach involves organizing a
competition to achieve the most admirable, interesting, and educational
experience—in other words, the most Brilliant Failure. Awarding a prize
to the most valuable or inspiring learning experience can advance the understanding of the importance of this discussion for the environment in
question and may at the same time help in collecting cases to illustrate and
further develop the starting points.

Such a project can be organized within a single organization, but it can
also be organized on a larger scale, such as within a sector.

206

Brilliant Failure Award Development Cooperation

For several years, the Institute of Brilliant Failures, in collaboration with the organization Spark and the Netherlands Ministry of Foreign Affairs, awarded a prize to the most Brilliant Failure in development cooperation. The core idea here was that it's unreasonable to expect all development aid activities to immediately achieve their desired results in environments where chaos and misery reign or used to reign, such as war, disease (Ebola), natural disasters (tsunamis, hurricanes, earthquakes) and poverty. Despite this, we're very critical when it comes to the effective use of our contributions, especially donations. This makes sense, but it definitely shouldn't make aid workers feel paralyzed and no longer able to provide the crucial yet risky support they provide. The organizations and employees involved, often volunteers, are involved because they want to make the world a better place. Do we really want these parties to feel unnecessarily threatened by us, the people largely watching from the comfort of our own homes?

   We certainly encountered resistance at first. Communication departments in particular were very reluctant to respond to the question of whether their organizations had any Brilliant Failures to share with us, fearful as they were of reputational damage. If it became known that aid projects can actually fail, potentially costing money, it would be widely reported in the press, evoking reactions from the public and politicians which couldresult in funding being cut, for example. Organizations were perfectly willing to send in their annual reports—but these, of course, didn't contain their Brilliant Failures... It's inspiring to mention that over time, it became easier to find examples. Now there are even NGOs that include their failures in their annual reports to prove they don't avoid complexity and potential failures in their efforts to solve difficult problems. Because if they don't, who will?

COOCENKI winner Brilliant Failure Award Development Cooperation 2010

The intention
COOCENKI (the *Coopérative Centrale du Nord-Kivu Congo*) is a union of 25 village cooperatives responsible for marketing the agricultural products of these cooperatives. In the late nineties, the cooperatives didn't have the liquid assets necessary to organize the buying and collecting of their member farmers' produce. The marketing was very inefficient as a result. This is why the Belgian NGO Vredeseilanden decided to make credit capital available.

The approach: First attempt
Vredeseilanden made available a thousand dollars per village cooperative. During the period 1998–2002, COOCENKI received financial support in the form of credit capital from Vredeseilanden, among others, to extend loans to its village cooperatives for buying and marketing their member farmers' produce during harvest season. These loans amounted to several thousand dollars per village cooperative.

The result
Having never managed such large amounts of money, the cooperatives were unable to pay them back. The original credit capital vanished into thin air.

The approach: Second attempt
An agent was appointed to visit the cooperatives and give them the money on the spot. Correct delivery of agricultural products often didn't take place. After several years of non-payment, COOCENKI stopped providing the loans and decided to recruit its own agent to visit the cooperatives

with the money and give them an amount that exactly mat-
ched the amount of produce collected.

The result
The man blindly believed that a certain amount of beans or
corn was available "nearby." Because he couldn't be everywhere at once, and couldn't return to the same place very
often, he repeatedly took the farmers at their word and paid
them the corresponding amount of money, but the correct
amount of produce was never fully delivered.

The approach: Third attempt
An entirely new credit system was put in place, based on
savings, order forms, and reimbursement by COOCENKI
upon delivery. The whole system was reconsidered and a
new formula was devised. A village cooperative now informs
COOCENKI when it can collect a certain amount of produce.
COOCENKI subsequently fills out an order form for the
amount specified. The village cooperative then takes this
order form to the local savings and credit cooperative. The
local savings and credit cooperative verifies the veracity of
the order form with COOCENKI staff and provides the necessary credit based on the locals' savings. The cooperative
uses this to pay the member farmers and organize transport
to the central warehouse. COOCENKI subsequently pays for
the produce, allowing the cooperative to repay its loan. It's a
win-win situation all around: The credit cooperative receives
interest on a short-term loan; the village cooperative markets the produce quickly, effectively, and independently; and
COOCENKI reduces its risks and increases its efficiency by
saving on follow-up costs.

The lessons learned

It's possible to sustainably set up large-scale commercial transactions without foreign support. Because the money came from abroad and was seen as a collective, anonymous debt, no one really felt responsible for managing it well and it wasn't paid back correctly. Now, after the first failures, the money is paid back to an autonomous and locally embedded organization providing credit based on the farmers and their neighbors' savings. There are no problems whatsoever with payback.

The debt from the first period hasn't been waived. COO-CENKI has, however, set up a help desk to encourage failing debtors to take new initiatives and support them in making these new activities profitable so they can use the profits to pay off their debts. But the most important learning experience was undoubtedly that it proved possible to use local resources to sustainably set up large-scale commercial trans-actions without foreign support—to this day. No one would'-ve discovered this if it hadn't been for the Brilliant Failure that occurred ten years ago.

Since 2007, COOCENKI has been supplying the UN World Food Programme with large quantities of beans and corn flour several times a year. They would never have managed to do so without an efficient purchasing system.

And there's more...

The learning effect has spread far and wide, especially in the area of policy and strategy, not just for COOCENKI/Vredesei-landen but for many development agencies. This is because many development agencies have encountered this particu-lar failure. The most important learning experience is that the local population doesn't take loans from foreign NGOs seriously because these NGOs aren't official banks or credit unions.

Brilliant Failure Award Healthcare

The healthcare industry is another, very important industry in which learning how to deal with failures adds an enormous amount of value. Innovation in healthcare is very difficult. This is mainly because the industry is incredibly complex, with extensive legislation and regulation, financial models, different organizations with different interests, and rapidly developing medical science and technology. It's an extensive and diverse field; more often than not, many—if not all—stakeholders are involved in an innovation, from patients, healthcare providers, institution managers and the government, to science and technology. A complicating factor is the fact that errors in the medical field are often associated with patient safety. An error can quickly lead to a health risk, which could even become a possible cause of death. It's no wonder, then, that the industry environment is characterized by risk aversion. There are also few incentives in the healthcare system that reward parties for taking risks and sharing any lessons learned with others. In short, there are plenty of reasons why it's a good idea to set up a healthcare industry program to reduce unnecessary risk-averse behavior and improve learning ability. The evolutionary metaphor that has been used for this is "the healthcare industry as an evolving system". This should lead to experimentation wherever possible and to both positive and negative outcomes being valued, shared, and applied. In order for such an approach to succeed, the involvement and support of a number of influential parties is required. In this case, these are provided through the Netherlands Ministry of Health, Welfare and Sport and project assurance is provided by the Netherlands Organization for Health Research and Development (ZonMw).

As stated previously, awarding a prize to the most valuable or inspiring learning experience can advance the understanding of the importance of this discussion for the environment in question and may at the same time help in collecting cases to illustrate and further develop the starting points. Focusing on social impact is important here. A good example of this is the winner of the Brilliant Failure Award Healthcare 2014.

The Brilliant Failures Award Healthcare 2014: Embolization Instead of Surgery

In 1995, a new method was described to treat people with uterine fibroids, benign tumors in the muscle tissue of the uterus. This alternative treatment renders surgical intervention unnecessary. The blood vessels supplying the fibroids with nutrients and oxygen are blocked with small synthetic particles, stopping the blood flow and causing the fibroids to shrink. The so-called EMMY ("embolization versus hysterectomy") trial of the Academic Medical Center of the University of Amsterdam (AMC) showed that uterine artery embolization has advantages over surgery: Hospital stay is shorter and recovery is faster. Because of this, uterine artery embolization is considerably cheaper. Quality of life after both interventions is equal, in the long term as well.

Professor Jim Reekers, a researcher and interventional radiologist at the AMC, set up a randomized multicenter study and found enough patients willing to participate. The study showed that embolization is clinically equivalent to surgery, but does offer significant advantages to the patient (see Hehenkamp et al. (2004)). This study, which was completed in 2005, earned Reekers the ZonMw Pearl, a prize awarded to remarkable research related to current developments whose results can easily be implemented.

Funded by the Dutch Foundation for Quality Funding for Medical Specialists, the professional association of gynecologists subsequently changed its guidelines: Uterine artery embolization now had to be discussed with each patient as an alternative to surgery. The ensuing silence was deafening. Despite all efforts to implement the new treatment, little has changed in practice. Each year approximately five thousand patients with uterine fibroids undergo surgery in the Netherlands, while only two hundred patients undergo uterine artery embolization.

According to Reekers, the main reason for this is that uterine artery embolization is performed by radiologists. Patients need to be referred to them by their gynecologist colleagues. But this isn't happening. Reekers: "Medical specialists have a protect-your-turf mentality—or, to use a polite euphemism, 'professional autonomy.' In plain language: don't touch my patients. Sometimes it's about money, but that's not the case in university hospitals, where specialists are on the payroll. Other interests are at play there. For example, there are surgeons in training who need to learn how to operate." Reekers only knows of one example where it does work: in the Dutch city of Tilburg, radiologists and gynecologists started working together to offer uterine artery embolization years ago. "They share a medical practice, splitting the profits. Together, they perform almost as many uterine artery embolization procedures (two hundred) as the rest of the Netherlands combined."

This story dates from 2014. A real effort has since been made to implement the new guidelines to ensure patients always receive the most appropriate treatment. Although it still happens that a hysterectomy procedure is performed where uterine artery embolization might have been a better choice, this is becoming less common.

You may be wondering how "brilliant" this failure is. Weren't these problems caused by healthcare providers depriving their patients of the best possible care? First of all, we don't know the extent to which this was done deliberately—but it's more important to consider the story from the perspective of the promotor of uterine artery embolization in the Netherlands. The approach worked in his practice and was proven appropriate for many other cases. However, it didn't just have to work in a controlled pilot environment or in a hospital where it fit within the business and/or financial model. It also had to work within the complex healthcare system in the Netherlands, including its sometimes perverse financial or other incentives. This situation could be compared to the innovation wisdom "a proof of concept is not a proof of business." Or, to stick with our Brilliant Failure archetypes: Beware of the Bear's Skin. This was the winning nomination because its BriFa score, V x I x R x A x L, was high, according to the jury:

- V (the value of the vision) was high; it's about an alternative to an invasive procedure, which could be of much value to patients. The alternative is also cheaper than the traditional treatment for uterine fibroids.
- I (inspiration or commitment) was very high.
- R (risk management) was high; it's about a difficult medical condition, and you can't know in advance whether the treatment will work satisfactorily in the longer term.
- A (approach) was high; the treatment was developed and performed with care and its effects were extensively studied.
- L (learning experiences) was high; lessons were learned about the new treatment, but ultimately also about the complex healthcare system with all its interests, incentives and habits.

This example also shows the importance of determining the impact from multiple perspectives when it comes to innovations involving multiple stakeholders. This idea is described in the archetype of the Empty Seat at the Table, which is relatively dominant in the healthcare industry. Another prevalent archetype is the Wrong Wallet, which is also at play here. The complex financing of the Dutch healthcare system regularly stifles innovation. The parties necessary to achieve success sometimes don't financially benefit from this success or even lose money on it. This phenomenon is especially evident when innovations are scaled up, involving the transition from proof of concept to proof of business, as described in the 2017 Interdepartmental Policy Report (IBO) on innovation in the Dutch healthcare industry. Scaling up often requires larger investments to be made and parties to jointly meet healthcare needs in a different and sustainable way, which not all parties will immediately be interested in. The party responsible for the system has to do something about this. But then, who is the responsible party?

IoBF Intervention: "Awareness Climate" for Experimentation and Learning

As discussed at various points in this book, the environment plays an important role in accepting and learning from unexpected and/or undesired developments. Brilliant Failures can only be valuable if people and organizations are given enough room to explore the world and learn from all experiences.

The IoBF Climate Scan is intended to provide an overview of the various factors that influence the room for experimentation and learning in a given environment. It has been applied to various environments and repeatedly led to concrete actions based on new insights into the "failure DNA" of the environments in question. The Scan contains three phases of self-assessment questions.

A. Experimenting

The first part is about the room for experimentation, trial (and error!), and entrepreneurship in the environment.

1. How often are you confronted with activities and/or projects that go differently than expected?
2. What is the ratio of "routine" versus "improvisation" in your activities?
3. Are you aware of the risks at the time of acting?
4. Do you have a clear idea of which risks of your actions and decisions are acceptable and which risks aren't acceptable?
5. To what extent do you experience the freedom to take risks?
6. If you've been involved in an activity or project that was stopped or didn't produce the desired results, did this mean you subsequently experienced difficulty getting involved in new activities?

B. Learning

The next part is about learning from experiences—both positive and negative experiences.

7. I learn from all my experiences.
8. I learn from the experiences of others.
9. Others learn from my experiences.
10. What is the ratio of "learning from failures" versus "learning from successes" in the environment?

C. Evolving

The next part is about internalizing and applying knowledge.

11. To what extent are learning experiences used to consider how things could or should be done differently?
12. How often have new insights led to changes in your approach?
13. How often have new insights led to changes in the parties you're involved with?
14. To what extent does knowledge get lost over time?

 **Applying Chapter 10**

Send in your own Brilliant Failure by scanning the QR code on the right or visiting www.briljantemislukkingen.en/ share-failure/ and clicking the "Share Your Brilliant Failure" button.

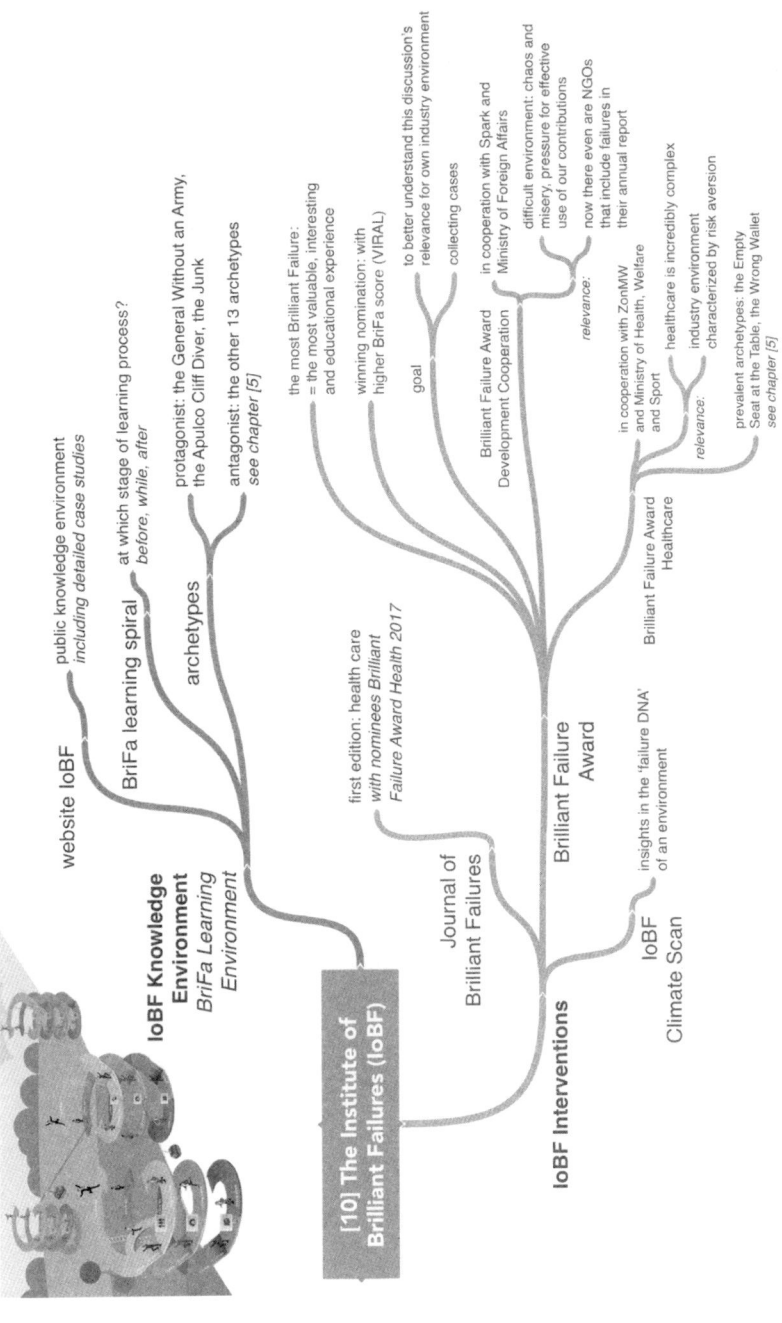

[10] The Institute of Brilliant Failures (IoBF)

IoBF Knowledge Environment
BriFa Learning Environment

- website IoBF
  - public knowledge environment
  - *including detailed case studies*
- BriFa learning spiral
  - at which stage of learning process?
  - *before, while, after*
- archetypes
  - protagonist: the General Without an Army, the Apulco Cliff Diver, the Junk
  - antagonist: the other 13 archetypes
  - *see chapter [5]*

Journal of Brilliant Failures

- first edition: health care *with nominees Brilliant Failure Award Health 2017*

Brilliant Failure Award

- the most Brilliant Failure: = the most valuable, interesting and educational experience
- winning nomination: with higher BriFa score (VIRAL)
- goal
  - to better understand this discussion's relevance for own industry environment
  - collecting cases
- Brilliant Failure Award Development Cooperation
  - in cooperation with Spark and Ministry of Foreign Affairs
  - *relevance:*
    - difficult environment: chaos and misery; pressure for effective use of our contributions
    - now there are NGOs that include failures in their annual report
- Brilliant Failure Award Healthcare
  - in cooperation with ZonMW and Ministry of Health, Welfare and Sport
  - *relevance:*
    - healthcare is incredibly complex industry environment characterized by risk aversion
    - prevalent archetypes: the Empty Seat at the Table, the Wrong Wallet *see chapter [5]*

IoBF Interventions

- IoBF Climate Scan
  - insights in the 'failure DNA' of an environment

ACKNOWLEDGMENTS

In accordance with the principle of Failing Brilliantly, the process of how this book came to be was one of trial and error rather than a linear process. Fortunately, I received much support along the way, and sometimes others helped me find a straight stretch of highway to speed down. I'm especially grateful to Bas Ruyssenaars, my loyal business partner at the Institute of Brilliant Failures from the very beginning, and Jildou de Jong, an unexpected godsend who planned to spend a few months working in an inspiring environment, but actually ended up providing much of that inspiration herself. I'm also thankful to my other colleagues at the Institute of Brilliant Failures, Florien, Quirine and Mirjam, for their contributions and commitment.

My thanks go out to those who have always supported the Institute of Brilliant Failures, such as the (then) Executive Board of ABN AMRO Bank (particularly Wietze Reehoorn and Johan van Hall), Henk Smid, director at ZonMW, and Erik Gerritsen, Director General at the Netherlands Ministry of Health, Welfare and Sport, both of whom recognize the importance of learning from Brilliant Failures in healthcare.

I'd also like to thank all guest authors and interviewees for the insights they have shared. Their contributions are great sources of inspiration and wisdom that can help us keep going and appreciate insights from the past that can be reused in the future.

I owe much gratitude to my Dutch publisher, Business Contact, particularly Janine Sloof and Sandra Wouters, for their unwavering trust in the production of this book and their valuable advice on matters of text and content.

Finally, of course, a word of thanks to my family. It may be interesting to know that I met my wife as a result of a Brilliant Failure. In October 1990 I was taking a short course at a training center near the city of Leiden, the Netherlands. I visited Leiden one Thursday evening, after another plan fell through because of bad weather. After the stores had closed I walked past a bar on my way back to my car. It looked nice, so I went inside—my first time visiting such an establishment, by the way. Once inside, I was offered a free drink several times. I eventually asked a young lady whether this was normal, in response to which she asked me if I hadn't been invited. It turned out that I was crashing a private birthday party thrown by three people, so no one had realized I wasn't supposed to be there. The young lady I'd approached was one of the hosts. When I got home, I decided to wish her a happy birthday by sending her flowers. To make a long story short: 2018 marks our 25th anniversary. In these 25 years we've been through a lot and, perhaps more than most, have seen the importance of honoring the past and focusing on a future in which the past is given the place it deserves. Hanna (my wife), Mirjam, Anne-Sophie and Louis fully support my work at the Institute of Brilliant Failures, even when I'm out and about or sitting in front of my computer again to think, talk, or write about Brilliant Failures. They, too, understand that it's all about the "brilliant," like the star that will always guide me.

Oostzaan, February 2019

GUEST AUTHORS

Sander Bais: Sander Bais is a professor of Theoretical Physics at the University of Amsterdam and an External Faculty Member at the Santa Fe Institute.

Marc Benninga: Marc Benninga is a professor of Pediatrics, specifically Pediatric Gastroenterology and Hepatology. His research focus on obstipation has earned him the nickname "The Poop Doctor." Marc previously played for the Netherlands men's national field hockey team.

Truls Berg: Truls Berg is a Norwegian Internet entrepreneur. He's the founder of the Open Innovation Lab of Norway (OIL) and publisher of *Innomag*, a Norwegian magazine about innovation and entrepreneurship.

Marcelis Boereboom: Marcelis Boereboom served as Director-General at the Netherlands Ministry of Health, Welfare and Sport until 2013, after which he served as Director-General and Acting Secretary-General at the Netherlands Ministry of Social Affairs and Employment. He currently serves as Director-General at the Netherlands Ministry of Education, Culture and Science.

Boohwan Byun: Boohwan Byun serves as Country Risk Manager at the Dutch ABN AMRO Bank. He's also a Visiting Professor at the Graduate School of Management of Technology and Vice President of the Korean Society in the Netherlands.

Maarten Camps: Maarten Camps has been serving as Secretary-General at the Netherlands Ministry of Economic Affairs and Climate Policy since August 2013. He previously held high positions at the Netherlands Ministry of Finance and the Netherlands Ministry of Social Affairs and Employment.

Jasmine Chang: Jasmine Chang holds a master's degree in Knowledge & Information Management and an MBA in Human Resource Management. She's the founder and manager of MAX HRM, a one-stop service provider of HR solutions for Chinese businesses in Belgium, the Netherlands and Luxembourg.

Rik Elgersma: Rik Elgersma serves as Director of Strategic Analysis at FrieslandCampina, one of the world's largest dairy companies. He regularly writes, speaks, and teaches at universities and seminars on such topics as data analysis and business intelligence in the areas of strategic analysis and competitive strategy.

Tonny Eyk: Tonny Eyk is a composer, accordionist, pianist, orchestra leader, producer and writer whose career in theater, film, radio and television spans more than fifty years. He has released more than 45 solo albums with various record labels and composed various tunes and jingles for various Dutch TV shows.

Erik Gerritsen: Erik Gerritsen currently serves as Secretary-General at the Netherlands Ministry of Health, Welfare and Sport. He previously served as general director at the Dutch Bureau for Youth Care, Agglomerate Amsterdam, and served as general director at Youth Protection, Amsterdam Region, from 2014 to 2015.

Foppe de Haan: Foppe de Haan served as head coach of Dutch soccer club SC Heerenveen for many years. He has also served as national coach of the Netherlands Under-21 team, which won the UEFA European U21 Championship in 2006 and 2007. Foppe was serving as assistant coach of the Netherlands women's national soccer team when it won the UEFA European Women's Championship 2017, which was hosted in the Netherlands.

Emiel Hanekamp: Emiel Hanekamp helps companies and governments achieve their energy and climate goals by providing insight into opportunities and reducing risks. Many of his projects focus on the transition to sustainable energy in developing countries.

Elizabeth Kleinveld: Elizabeth Kleinveld is a start-up matchmaker and angel investor. She's also an artist and photographer, dividing her time between Amsterdam and New Orleans. In her art she strives for creative self-expression, responding to what she observes in the world.

Bennie Mols: Bennie Mols is a science journalist specializing in robots, artificial intelligence, and the human brain. He has authored such books as *Turings tango. Waarom de mens de computer de baas blijft* [*Turing's Tango: Why Computer Intelligence Will Never Exceed Human Intelligence*] and *Hallo robot. De machine als medemens* [*Hello Robot: Machine as Man*].

Henk Oosterling: Henk Oosterling is an associate professor in Philosophy at Erasmus University Rotterdam. He's also a former Dutch national Kendo champion. His latest book *Waar geen wil is, is een weg* [*Where There's No Will, There's a Way*] promotes intercultural "action thinking," a philosophy Oosterling applies to his educational projects in the city of Rotterdam.

Ger Post: Ger Post studied journalism and cognitive neuroscience and currently teaches in the master's program Brain and Cognitive Sciences at the University of Amsterdam. In addition to textbooks on interdisciplinary research, he writes articles on brain research for such magazines as *De Neuroloog* [*The Neurologist*] and *Managementboek Magazine* [*Management Book Magazine*].

Wim de Ridder: Wim de Ridder is a futurist and was a professor of Future Research at the University of Twente from 2002 to 2015. He served as director of the Society and Enterprise Foundation, a corporate think tank in the Netherlands, from 1983 to 2007.

Frank Rozemeijer: Frank Rozemeijer holds the NEVI Chair in Purchasing and Supply Chain Management at the Maastricht University School of Business and Economics, teaching and researching topics such as social capital in supply chains. Since 2004, he's had his own business providing consultancy services, training courses, and executive coaching.

Bas Ruyssenaars: Bas Ruyssenaars is co-founder of The Institute of Brilliant Failures and founder of the strategy agency De Keuze Architecten [The Choice Architects], which develops interventions for "simplifying choosing and triggering new behavior." He also invented the innovative sports game YOU.FO.

Hans Steensma: Hans Steensma is a reservist platoon commander in the Royal Netherlands Marine Corps (RNLMC) and co-founder of the Military Formats in Business Group (MFIB). Since 2007, he and Erik Elgersma have been applying military formats in a business context, for example by organizing war games in various countries and scouting and training war-game operators.

Theo van der Tak: Theo van der Tak served as a partner at the organizational consultancy firm Twynstra, where he was specialized in supervising managers and employees in implementing and executing program management. He has worked with various Dutch ministries, municipalities, and provinces. He co-authored the book *Program Canvas: Samen naar de kern van je programma* [*Program Canvas: Getting to the Core of Your Program Together*].

Tjark Tjin-A-Tsoi: Tjark Tjin-A-Tsoi serves as Director General at Statistics Netherlands (CBS). He previously served as CEO of the Netherlands Forensic Institute. Before that, he held positions at companies such as the Netherlands Competition Authority, Ernst & Young, Rabobank, and Royal Dutch Shell.

Mathieu Weggeman: Mathieu Weggeman is a professor of Organization Science, specifically Innovation Management, at the Eindhoven University of Technology. He has his own consultancy business, advising on such matters as the design and management of knowledge-intensive organizations.

Martijn van Westerop: Martijn van Westerop is a founding partner of the International Sports Management Academy, executive coach at IMD in Lausanne, Switzerland, lecturer in the master's program Advanced Studies in Sport Administration & Technology at the International Academy of Sport Science and Technology (AISTS) in Lausanne, and professor at the Johan Cruyff Institute. He previously played for the Netherlands men's national field hockey team.

REFERENCES

ABN AMRO Bank and the Netherlands Ministry of Economic Affairs (2006). *Tweede kans. Lessen in vallen en opstaan* [*Second Chance. Lessons in Trial and Error*]. Dialogues.

Altshuller, G.S. & R. Shapiro (1956), "About a Technology of Creativity", *Questions of Psychology*, No. 6, pp. 37–49.

Andel, Pek van & Brands, Wim (2014). *Serendipiteit: de Ongezochte Vondst* [*Serendipity: The Unsought Discovery*]. Nieuw Amsterdam, Amsterdam.

Ansoff, H. Igor (2007). Strategic Management Classic. Palgrave Macmillan, Hampshire.

Argyris, C. & Schön, D. (1978). *Organizational Learning: A Theory of Action Perspective*. Addison-Wesley, Reading.

Baker, Randolph & Gower, Kim (2010). "Strategic Application of Story-telling in Organizations: Toward Effective Communication in a Diverse World", *Journal of Business Communication,* Vol. 47, No. 3, pp. 295–312.

Bammens, Y., Gils, A. van & Voordeckers, W. (2010). "The Role of Family Involvement in Fostering an Innovation-Supportive Stewardship Culture", Academy of Management Best Paper Proceedings.

Bar-Yam, Yaneer (2002). *Complexity Rising: From Human Beings to Human Civilization, a Complexity Profile*. New England Complex Systems Institute, Cambridge.

Benyus, Janine M. (1998). *Biomimicry: Innovation Inspired by Nature*. Harper Perennial, New York.

Blom, Robert (2004). *Faillissement. Oorzaak en gevolg* [*Bankruptcy. Cause and Effect*]. Graydon, ISBN Amsterdam.

Boston Consulting Group (2002). *Setting the Phoenix Free: A Report on Entrepreneurial Restarters*. The Boston Consulting Group GMBH, Munich.

Brafman, Ori & Brafman, Rom (2010). *Onderstroom, de onweerstaanbare drang tot irrationeel gedrag* [*Sway: The Irresistible Pull of Irrational Behavior*]. Maven Publishing, Amsterdam.

Camps, Maarten (2017). "Durf te leren" ["Dare to Learn"], *ESB*, January.

Chesbrough, H. (2003). *Open Innovation: The New Imperative for Creating and Profiting from Technology*. Harvard Business School Press, Boston.

Crane, F.G. & Crane, E.C. (2007). "Dispositional Optimism and Entrepreneurial Success", *The Psychologist-Manager Journal, 10*(1), pp. 13–25.

Crutzen, Paul & Stoermer, Eugene (2000). "The Anthropocene", *Global Change Newsletter IGBP, 41*, pp. 17–18.

De Bono, Edward (1955). *Serious Creativity: Using the Power of Lateral Thinking to Create New Ideas*. HarperCollins Publishers, London.

Denning, Stephen (2000). *The Springboard. How Storytelling Ignites Action in Knowledge-Era Organizations*. Taylor and Francis Ltd., Abingdon.

Dimitrova, N.G. (2014). "Rethinking Errors: How Error-Handling Strategy Affects Our Thoughts and Others' Thoughts About Us", *PhD Thesis*, Vrije Universiteit Amsterdam.

Duijvenvoorde, Anna C.K. van, Zanolie, Kiki, Rombouts, Serge A.R.B., Raijmakers, Maartje E.J. & Crone, Eveline A. (2008). "Evaluating the Negative or Valuing the Positive? Neural Mechanisms Supporting Feedback-Based Learning Across Development", *The Journal of Neuroscience*, 28(38), pp. 9495–9503.

Edmondson, Amy (1999). "Psychological Safety and Learning Behavior in Work Teams", *Administrative Science Quarterly*, Vol. 44, No. 2, pp. 350–383.

Erasmus Innovatie Monitor (2015), http://cdn2.hubspot.net hubfs/552232/Erasmus_Innovatiemonitor_2015_onderzoeksrapport.pdf?t=1447940880942.

Haushofer, Johannes (2016). "CV of Failures", www.princeton.edu/~joha/Johannes_Haushofer_CV_of_Failures.pdf.

Henderson, R. & Clark K. (1990). "Architectural Innovation: The Reconfiguration of Existing Product Technologies and the Failure of Established Firms", *Administrative Science Quarterly*, Vol 35, No. 1. Special Issue: Technology, Organizations and Innovation.

Hmieleski, K.M. & Baron, R.A. (2009). "Entrepreneurs' Optimism and New Venture Performance: A Social Cognitive Perspective", *Academy of Management Journal, 52*(3), pp. 473–488.

Hofstede, Geert (1994). *Cultures and Organizations*. Profile Books, London.

IBO Innovatie in de zorg [Interdepartmental Policy Report (IBO) on Innovation in the Healthcare Industry] (2017), www.rijksoverheid.nl/documenten/rapporten/2017/04/24/ibo-innovatie-in-de-zorg.

Iske, Paul (2016). *Combinatorische Innovatie [Combinatoric Innovation]*. SMO, Rotterdam.

Iske, Paul (ed.) (2017). "De Zorg als Evoluerend Systeem: het belang van Briljante Mislukkingen" ["The Healthcare Industry as an Evolving System: The Importance of Brilliant Failures"], *Nederlands Tijdschrift voor Briljante Mislukkingen – Editie Zorg* [*Dutch Journal of Brilliant Failures – Healthcare Issue*], *No.1,* December.

Kahneman, Daniel & Tversky, Amos (2012). *Ons feilbare denken* [*Thinking, Fast and Slow*], Business Contact, Amsterdam.

Kauffman, Stuart & Johnsen, S. (1991). "Co-Evolution to the Edge of Chaos: Coupled Fitness Landscapes, Poised States, and Co-Evolutionary Avalanches", *Journal of Theoretical Biology* 149, pp. 467–505.

Kauffman, Stuart (1995). *At Home in the Universe: The Search for the Laws of Self Organization and Complexity.* Oxford University Press, Oxford.

Kelling, George L. & Wilson, James Q. (1992). "Broken Windows: The Police and Neighborhood Safety", *The Atlantic Monthly,* March.

Klein, G. (2007). "Performing a Project Premortem", *Harvard Business Review* 85 (9), pp. 18–19.

Kolb, D.A. (1984). *Experiential Learning: Experience as the Source of Learning and Development.* Prentice Hall, Englewood Cliffs.

Land, George & Beth, Jarman (1992). *Breakpoint and Beyond: Mastering the Future Today.* HarperBusiness, New York.

Leadbeater, Charles (2000). "Innovation: Survival of the Fittest", *Accenture Outlook Journal Quaterly* 18 (3), pp. 307–343.

Leenders, M.R. & Fearon, H.R., (2008). "Developing Purchasing's Foundation", *Journal of Supply Chain Management,* Vol. 44, Issue 2, pp. 17–27.

Luthans, F. & Youssef, C.M. (2004), "Human, Social, and Now Positive Psychological Capital Management", *Organizational Dynamics, 33*(2), pp. 143–160.

Luthans, F., Avolio, B.J., Avey, J.B. & Norman, S.M. (2007). "Positive Psychological Capital: Measurement and Relationship with Performance and Satisfaction", *Personnel Psychology, 60*(3), pp. 541–572.

Mager, Birgit (2011), "Enthusiasm. Touchpoint", *Journal of Service Design,* Vol. 2, No. 3, pp. 30–31.

Mitchell, Melanie (2011). *Complexity: A Guided Tour.* Oxford University Press, Oxford.

Parkhurst, Howard (1999). "Confusion, Lack of Consensus, and the Definition of Creativity as a Construct", *The Journal of Creative Behavior*, Vol. 33, No. 1, pp. 1–21.

Parkinson, Cyrill Northcote (1955). "Parkinson's Law", *The Economist*, November.

Peterson, C. (2000). "The Future of Optimism", *American Psychologist, 55*(1), pp. 44–55.

Ries, Eric (2017). *De startup-methode* [*The Start-Up Method*], Business Contact, Amsterdam.

Rifkin, Jeremy (2005). *The European Dream*. Wiley, Hoboken.

Röskes, Carsten (2017). "Factors Affecting the Survival of Gazelles and Other High-Growth Companies", Master Thesis Maastricht University.

Scharmer, Otto (2009). *Theory U: Leading from the Future as it Emerges*. SoL, the Society for Organizational Learning, Cambridge.

Scheier, M.F. & Carver, C.S. (1993). "On the Power of Positive Thinking: The Benefits of Being Optimistic", *Current Directions in Psychological Science, 2*(1), pp. 26–30.

Schneider, S.L. (2001). "In Search of Realistic Optimism. Meaning, Knowledge, and Warm Fuzziness", *The American Psychologist, 56*(3), pp. 250–263.

Schoemaker, P.H.J. (2011). *Brilliant Mistakes: Finding Success on the Far Side of Failure*. Wharton Digital Press, Philadelphia.

Schumpeter, J.A. (1912/1934). *The Theory of Economic Development*. Harvard University Press, Cambridge.

Seligman, M., Ernst, R., Gillhamc, J., Reivicha, K. & Linkinsd, M. (2009). "Positive education: Positive Psychology and Classroom Interventions", *Oxford Review of Education*, Vol. 35, No. 3, pp. 293–311.

Sitkin, Sim B. (1992). "Learning Through Failure: The strategy of Small Losses", *Research in Organizational Behavior*, Vol. 14, pp. 231–266.

Strack, S., Carver, C.S. & Blaney, P. H. (1987). "Predicting Successful Completion of an Aftercare Program Following Treatment for Alcoholism: The Role of Dispositional Optimism", *Journal of Personality and Social Psychology, 53*(3), pp. 579–584.

Taleb, Nassim Nicholas (2008). *The Black Swan: The Impact of the Highly Improbable*. Penguin Books, London.

Weggeman, Mathieu (1997). *Kennismanagement* [*Knowledge Management*]. Scriptum, Schiedam.

Wynstra, J.Y.F. (2006). "Inkoop, Leveranciers en Innovatie: van VOC tot Space Shuttle" ["Procurement, Suppliers and Innovation: From the Dutch East India Company (VOC) to the Space Shuttle"], *Inaugural Address*, ERIM Erasmus Research Institute of Management, Rotterdam, pp. 48–49.

Websites

Apptimism: www.apptimism.eu.

Institute of Brilliant Failures: www.brilliantfailures.com.

International Institute for Serious Optimism: www.iiso.eu.